Dirty Little Tricks

How Salespeople Are Robbing You Blind!

About The Author

Thomas Ray Crowel has been a salesman his entire adult life. At ten years old, he sold hobby horses door-to-door. At twenty, his sales career began in earnest. He has special expertise in "cold" canvassing and has knocked on over 250,000 doors. This technique is considered the most difficult by professional sales representatives. Through his selling skills, he now holds his current position as head of three multi-million dollar sales organizations.

Tom graduated from Purdue University with a degree in clinical psychology and did graduate work at the University of Chicago. He is a life member of the American Association of Professional Hypnotherapists and a Certified Diplomate of The American Psychotherapy Association. For his humanity, wisdom, and leadership, he received the Sagamore of the Wabash Award—the highest honor the Governor of the

State of Indiana bestows on an individual.

A much sought-after speaker for motivational and sales seminars, Thomas' first book, **_Simple Selling: Common Sense That Guarantees Your Success_** continues to be a bestseller. Born and raised in Hammond, Indiana, Tom resides with his wife, Nancy, in nearby Highland, Indiana. His two sons, Thomas Gehrig and Robert Ray, are now his business partners. Thomas' calling is to help and guide the "salt of the earth," the common person. Both of his books, **_Simple Selling_** and **_Dirty Little Tricks_** are directed towards the "salt."

Dirty
Little
Tricks

How Salespeople Are Robbing You Blind!

by
Thomas Ray Crowel

Illustrations by
Patricia Ann Gillham

$ $uccess Press

Success Press, Highland, IN 46322
Copyright © 2000 by Thomas Ray Crowel

All rights reserved under International and Pan-American Copyright
Conventions. Published in the United States by Success Press,
Highland, IN 46322

Library of Congress Catalog Number: 00-90246

ISBN: 0-9669917-2-9

Acknowledgments

The research and writing of *Dirty Little Tricks: How Salespeople Are Robbing You Blind* has been a special "work" for me, mostly because I know it will help you, the reader, become better informed and more prepared the next time you encounter an unscrupulous sales rep. Over forty years of selling on the streets have taught me that no one makes it in life without the support and guidance of many others. In return, I'd like to thank those whose contributions have assisted me in taking this book from vision to reality.

To my late parents, Otis D. and Delphia E. Crowel, who shaped my character at a very young age. To Nancy, my wife and mother of my two sons, Tom and Bob, who are also my faithful business partners. My brother Larry and sister Marjorie, who have always been there for me. To Patricia Gillham, my publicist, who supports me and my efforts daily and without fail. To my company's manager, Pamela J. Ladwig, who is always an encouraging advocate. And to each of my company staff, whose dedication to minding the store has enabled me to "reinvent" myself into a published author.

There are many other individuals who contributed to this work, particularly the many true and sincere salespersons with whom I've crossed paths. Especially the ones who have stopped along the way to share a "sales tale" with me. And, finally, to you—the reader. You all make what I do profoundly gratifying and worthwhile.

Table of Contents

Preface

I decided to write ***Dirty Little Tricks: How Salespeople Are Robbing You Blind*** for three main reasons. The first reason, I'll have to admit, was to promote my first book, ***Simple Selling: Common Sense That Guarantees Your Success.***

To understand how ***Dirty Little Tricks*** would aid in getting publicity for increasing the sales of ***Simple Selling,*** you must realize that when promoting a book, one has to get as much exposure as possible. The best way to "hype" a book, of course, is through radio, television, and the internet. Of these, radio is a biggie. People listen to it while driving to and from work. They listen to talk radio while trying to fall asleep at night. When you give it some thought, you always see individuals with radios while jogging, sun bathing or driving home. Take a moment and think about it. Agreed? Good.

I realized that just about everyone successful at selling their books begin by doing radio gigs. It made sense to me, since almost everyone you see on popular television shows are celebrities. Since my goal was to spend much of my time sharing my message in **Simple Selling,** checking out one of the least expensive means of advertising but most effective, the radio talk show was something that I had to consider. However, it's not just a simple matter of going on a radio talk show and talking about one's book. In fact, your book's the last thing the producer and host are interested in. They naturally look forward to interviews that audiences find interesting. That's right...call-in talk shows are about ratings, not selling books.

So, as you can see, a book about selling that explains how honesty and knowledge are all you need to become successful, won't secure me a lot of radio show interviews. Yet talking about how everyday folks out in the business world are getting *gouged* might. After all, who likes to be cheated? I took a pencil and started writing down the times I could remember being scammed. This made for quite a long list. I even added to my list what others shared with me about their own bad experiences with salespeople. *Voila!* The birth of my radio and TV program: "Dirty Little Tricks: How Salespeople Are Robbing You Blind!"

One morning, as I was sitting at my desk at the office, I was proofing a radio ad an advertising company had put together for me. It had all the various "bullets," like: "How supermarkets trick you into buying impulse items." "The trick that car salespeople use to pique your interest in almost any car on the lot." "How a seemingly innocent mistake gas stations make could have you paying too much at the pump." You get the idea. But as I read on, I began doodling, and for some reason I was looking at a photo of myself and thinking: "I look too honest for this written script." At that moment I drew a mask over my eyes. It looked funny and resembled a cartoon. I showed it to my publicist. She laughed and we decided to send it to the advertising company. It was accepted immediately. After all, isn't a picture worth a thousand words? Furthermore, over all my years of selling, I have often heard a customer when talking about salespeople say: "All they need to be complete is a mask." Not the best commentary, but as you'll discover, true!

By "unmasking" many of the sales tricks, you will become a better buyer. I'm sure that at one time or another each of us has been on the short end of the stick. Maybe it's been a car salesman who sold you a "lemon" or just didn't deliver what he said he would. Don't just think of the automobile salesman as the only ones who are selling. You would be more correct if you considered almost *everyone* as a salesperson. Include merchants, doctors, lawyers, and, of course, politicians. People in general sell their own cars, houses and goods. Because I have spent my lifetime as a salesman, it hasn't been by accident that I have had people share their horror stories with me. Since I know of no book that covers such inside information, I'm sure you will become a better buyer. I'm going to share with you here some various "sales tricks" and tell how you can avoid them. Don't you agree that knowledge is power?

Let's take a look at time, money, and grief. Time is what you and I need to consider the most. It is a constant that you can never get back once spent. Whenever I think of an individual such as yourself reading my book or listening to me speak at a seminar, it's my privilege, because you have chosen to share time that you will never be able to retrieve again. Keep in mind that your time to you is just as important as anyone else's is to them. Later, I will show you how you can be spared being robbed of your time.

I'll also share experiences and information

that will save you money and give you peace of mind. Money is important to most of us because we need it to provide us with the comforts of life. However, money is not a constant, so no matter how important it can be to us, it's not as great as our loss of time.

Losing time and money can bring us grief. When we misplace or misuse our finances or time, we tend to be unhappy with ourselves. This, of course, causes mixed emotions. Now, if some-one else robs us of our money or time, we usually become even more angered. Who needs extra grief? So there you have it. This is what I'll be sharing with you...that is, how to deal with the salespeople who don't give a darn about you or your money. This is the best reason for this book!

Introduction

Being tricked or taken for a ride can be frivolous or harmful, depending on whether you lose money or your sanity. If you lose money, then I'm quite sure that your sanity will follow.

When individuals are made to look a fool, many emotions surface: anger, disappointment, humiliation, and others. When you are taken advantage of by a sales "rep," it takes awhile to get rid of the bad taste it leaves in your mouth. Of course the resentment you feel towards the salesperson usually increases in direct relationship to how much money or humiliation it cost you. For example, if a person happens to be a millionaire, losing a hundred dollars does not have the same effect as someone who is struggling to make ends meet. That hundred could represent badly needed food, clothing, or shelter. On the other hand, if an individual has more than sufficient funds, the loss of one hundred dollars could be the same as losing a few pennies.

Always keep in mind that monetary loss is only part of the loss. In fact, if you spend your time thinking about how and by whom you have been mistreated, it takes away from the more pleasant and productive thoughts that you should <u>really</u> be focusing on instead. Besides, when your thoughts keep turning to salespeople who screwed you over, you are allowing them to "get into" your head. They've already forgotten when they took advantage of you! You have allowed them "free rent" space in your head. In other words, *you're* most likely the only one experiencing mental anguish.

Since you alone know what "loss" means to you, as you read ***Dirty Little Tricks,*** the humor or sorrow will be for you to judge. Join me as I take you to the inner-sanctum of the masked sales reps, and reveal some of their scams. We'll look at some of their more infamous "tricks."

UN-MASK 'EM

In the illustrations there are 16 masks undercover

They're hidden for you to discover

As I wrote in my book

You might meet people who rob and crook

So when you spend your hard earned cash

Make certain what you get ain't just trash

You'll need the edge on your deals

So be on your toes and not your heels

If you don't find all the masks, don't fret

Visit our web-site at simpleselling.net

PART I:

Buying and Selling Tricks

Buying Goals

Since most individuals selling a product or service have <u>selling goals</u>, you should have buying goals when you are purchasing a product or service. It is in your favor that before you go "shopping," you should have a good idea of what your needs are, how much you are willing to spend, the knowledge it will require, and who you're doing business with. Buyers need to have goals as well as sellers, if they are going to be effective.

Step 1: Check out all the requirements you are looking for. If it's an automobile you're planning to purchase, make a list of what you definitely need and what you can do without. For example, jot down: "four door, automatic, AM/FM stereo, power steering, full size with air conditioning." However, color, make, or other extras, such as a CD-player, may make little or no difference to you.

Step 2: How much can you afford? Write it down! If your top limit is ten thousand dollars, make a note of it.

Step 3: Learn something about the car. Check out comparisons at various car lots. Get on the internet or go to the library and look at the *Consumer's Guide.* Ask librarians if they have a copy of the "Red Book" for automobiles.

Step 4: Ask family and friends if they know a dealer you can trust. Nothing beats a good recommendation. I use the automobile as an example because most of us at one time or another are in the market for one.

You may apply the same standards to most purchases or services. For instance, if it's a professional service you may need then ask yourself the same type of questions. When deciding on a physician, the things I would want to know are, "Do I need surgery or is there an alternative?" "Can I afford this?" (Don't be afraid to ask!). I can remember asking a doctor how much it was going to cost for my son to have surgery. He said, "Oh, don't worry about the cost. Let's just get the boy healthy." My reply was, "Well, Doctor, if it's going to cost a million dollars, then I'm going to have to consider other options." Never let someone try to intimidate you. By the way, after taking my son to another doctor, it was correctly decided that his operation was not needed.

You will find that almost any product or service you are seeking can be put into simple terms. The main thing is to *avoid impulse decision making*. Have a plan. Make yourself a "grocery list." Decide where, when, and who you will do business with, and, above all, recognize the tricks I will discuss.

Who Are These Sellers?

Almost one hundred percent of the time when I am doing a radio show on "Dirty Little Tricks: How Salespeople Are Robbing You

Blind!," the conversation will lead to the used car salesman. I always ask the host if I can state two facts before we begin the interview. **1.** Everyone, at one time or another, is a salesperson. **2.** Most people are honest.

Take a moment to give the sales process a thought and you will agree that almost everyone is trying to convince someone of something. Just as an automobile sales representative is trying to sell cars, others are "selling" their goods or services. To name a few: doctors, lawyers, preachers, educators, and politicians. All you have to do is look through the yellow pages in the phone book. There you will see their sales ads.

Furthermore, mothers and fathers are working on "selling" their kids good values, and their children are attempting to convince them on letting them have their own way on how late they can stay up, or how they would like to dress, to name a few.

As for honesty, if everyone had the same spell that Pinocchio had cast, there wouldn't be any need to write this book. Noses would grow right before our eyes! However, I did say there are many honest salespeople out there. All you need to do is look in the mirror and ask yourself if you are one of them. Don't worry about your nose growing, since the Pinocchio syndrome doesn't exist. Or does it? I call it the mask, and, I want to share with you some sales tricks that when avoided will save you money, time and grief.

Yellow Pagers

I consider everyone who is attempting to convince someone of something a salesperson. Even if they don't admit it. Even when they try to convince me they aren't. If you disagree with me, take me to the test. Open up the Yellow Pages. Now examine those pages from A to Z. Here's what you will discover. Advertising that reads selling, shopping, saving time, buying by phone, services, fulfilling needs—all this and more you'll find in the Yellow Pages. So now that we agree on this, we can move on and get back to those dirty little tricks. A cosmetic surgeon once took exception to being called a salesman by me. I was only attempting to convince him so that he could realize that the individuals he employs as "patient reps" should be trained to build patient relationships and meet their patient's needs. Then he could convince his clients that he <u>could</u> perform skilled surgery and assure them the procedure would turn out just fine. Sounds like selling to me. What do you think?

Sometimes the real sales job is to convince patients that <u>their</u> time is <u>not</u> as valuable as the physician's. Don't you ever believe it. Your time is as important to you as the doctor's is to him. That's why you should not be made to sit in a waiting room for hours on end. Wouldn't you gripe if a waiter had you wait too long before he served you? Since I believe your time is very important, I'm going to suggest throughout this book how you can solve the dreaded wait in professional offices.

To begin with, when you make your appointments, inform the receptionist that you only have so much time to spare. Arrange your appointments far enough in advance so that you won't find yourself in a last minute situation where you have to be squeezed in. By all means speak up! Ever heard the adage, "A squeaky wheel gets the oil."? As a result, most of the time you will have choices and options.

Retail "2-Fer-1"

I'm quite sure that all of you are aware of the "2-fer-1" items on sale. It seems as though these sales items are popping up just about everywhere. They can be found in most retail establishments and many times supermarkets display them at the end of their aisles.

Well, while shopping at one of the well-known "marts," I decided to buy a bag of peanuts as I was waiting by the check-out counter. The display sign read: "Two bags of peanuts for 1\frac{00}{}$!" I only wanted one bag, so I grabbed it and placed it on the counter. But when the clerk scanned the bag of peanuts, it came to 44¢. If I had purchased two bags, the total would have scanned 1\frac{00}{}$. Not the good deal you thought you'd get.

In order to be fair, sometimes the 2-fer-1's are a good buy. However, in many cases it's often a *break-even* for the buyer. The cost of a package of paper plates might sell for 1\frac{25}{}$, but they will be displayed "on sale" at four packages for 5^{00}. Same price, since four times 1^{25} <u>is</u> 5^{00}...no matter how you add it up.

When a store is doing a volume of business, these items add up to quite a profit. Of course profits and competition are what capitalism is all about. Just the same, the money is just as good in your capitalist pocket as it is in theirs.

Was/Nows

Here's another sales gimmick for you to consider. It's the "two price labels" on one item. Many times there <u>is</u> an actual bargain for the consumer. However, more than likely it's another scheme that merchants use in order to sell their goods.

Since this is such a widely used promotion by retailers, it's easy for the buyer not to give it a second thought. For example, while you're in a liquor store shopping for a bottle of your favorite wine, you may notice other bottles of wine with two price labels on them. One of the stickers may read eighteen dollars and the other, just barely covering the eighteen dollar label, is less. Twelve dollars, for instance. You may impulsively pick up the bottle of wine and put it in your shopping cart.

Before making these quick decisions, it would be a good idea to check around a few other stores. You might just find out that the cost of the same bottle of wine was *always* around twelve dollars. I'm sure you're aware of the adage: "It's not what you make but what you save." Some liquor stores use these *was/now* labels quite often.

However, so do many other stores. You can locate these *was/now* stickers on food, toys, tools, and almost any type of product you can imagine. Since this sales trick doesn't usually lead to bankruptcy, I won't belabor the point. Instead, I'll leave you with another old saying. A penny saved is a penny earned. I've always been a sucker for *was/now* labels. I am going to be more careful in the future. How about you?

"Double Tagged"

The *double tag scam*. Sooner or later you will come across the double tag on one of your shopping excursions. Here's the way it works.

While looking through a clothing rack in the department store, you see a sweater you like. You discover the sweater has two price tags. On one sleeve, the tag reads $49^{95}. However, on the other sleeve the ticket displays a cost of $39^{95}. You may say to yourself: "What's up with this?" That is, what is the correct price?

Since you are interested in purchasing the sweater, your next step would be to look around for a sales clerk and get the price difference settled. Since other sweaters on the rack are the same as the one in your hand except for size, they all have a price tag of $49^{95}. This makes you believe there's been an error made on the $39^{95} sweater. No need to worry yourself. The clerk already knows the answer. She was informed early on to place *both* tags on the sweater in question. See, the store is willing to sell <u>all</u> the sweaters for $39^{95}. The tag's a "come on."

When you explain the situation to the clerk, she scratches her head and exclaims: "There must be a mistake!" She further tells you since it's their (the store's) mistake, they will have to take the loss. That is, she will sell it to you for the lower tagged price. You're delighted and she's happy. You take your purchase and you are on your way.

Later on, another sweater will get another tag and the store snags another customer. After all, "accidents" can happen. What do you think? Have you been *double tagged* by this clever sales gimmick?

Rolling The Hole

Unfortunately this trick was told to me some years back by the proprietor of an ice cream parlor. He explained that when he hired people, he would demonstrate how to take an ice cream scooper and scoop out the ice cream to make it look like a big dip on the cone, but with a hole in the center. He took pride in the fact that it was a skill he could pass on while making a little more money by giving kids a little less ice cream.

Since discussing this "rolling the hole" with others, I came to find out that many soft-serve ice cream or yogurt stores have even found a way to increase their profits while duping the customer. Here's how it works. The server takes the cone and works the soft-serve on the edges, thereby leaving the cone empty. Pretty clever, eh? Do you think that's where the name "soda jerk" comes from? Why don't we just refer to them as jerks, period, when they pull this stunt?

Of course kids don't get all the gypping. There's plenty to go around. I remember the false bottom beer glass. I would order a schooner of beer at the neighborhood tavern. Some of us can still remember that when you were served a big schooner of beer, it was just that. Big. So I was rather surprised when picking up the glass to take a big drink only to find that it was half empty (or half full if you choose to be an optimist.) The bottom of the glass stem was just that—all glass.

The false bottom has spread quite well. You'll find the false shot glass, drinking glass, and of course don't forget the kids. They get the false bottom root beer mug. If you want your money's worth here, buy your drink in a bottle or can, then pour it directly into your own "mug."

In the candy industry there can definitely be benefits. For example, at one time candy companies made one size candy bar, maybe two. They were standard and large. Not today! Almost all candy companies have over the years downsized their product but kept the price the same. Let's look on the bright side. Years ago you would have asked your friend for a bite of their candy bar. Not today. The candy industry now produces the bite sized bar while taking a little bite out of your buck. Always compare the size with the price. Many times smaller is cheaper.

Of course giving less for more is catching on throughout the business world. For example, less material in many brands of shirts, suits, dresses and so on. Factories have now decided to cut down on <u>tailoring</u>. For example, a person can wear a size "large" shirt in one brand but will need an "extra large" in another. There's no consistency from one manufacturer to another in shirts, dresses or suits. If a manufacturer skimps on the material, the garment will be a tighter fit for the wearer but ultimately will bring the manufacturer more profits. So, we're getting rolled in many ways.

THE WALL STREET JOURNAL.

Thursday, June 17, 1999 *Joseph B. Cahill*
Staff Reporter

Sears Faces Another Suit On Auto Work

... The Sears automotive business has also been the subject of complaints that it foisted unneeded repairs on customers and passed off used car batteries as new. Sears paid $15 million to resolve a repair scandal in 1992 and earlier this year paid nearly $1 million to settle a probe of the battery sales in Florida. In neither case did Sears admit liability. ...

Batteries

Most of us are aware of that little pink rabbit who never runs out of energy in our TV commercial. How long or strong a small battery will last apparently makes no difference when it comes to name brand or generic brands. In fact, many generic brand batteries are manufactured by name brand companies. Therefore when purchasing small household batteries such as B, C, D, A, AA, AAA, buy the cheapest. Research proves that battery life is about the same, regardless of what company's name is on the package. An extra plus is that many of the "off brands" cost half the price of their name brand competition. Not the same story for automobile batteries however.

Not too long ago, *Dateline* televised a program on a major retail store re-selling used car batteries. Outside investigators were going undercover to find out if certain stores were re-selling used car batteries as new ones. I imagine that you have already guessed this one, even if you didn't see the program. The story proved out.

There were, in fact, stores selling used batteries as new ones. The investigators actually purchased the batteries, documented the serial numbers, returned them to the store and re-purchased them as new.

Make sure that when you purchase a car battery that there are no scratches on the posts. Also, try to have it tested by an outside source. It seems to me that this "shady" little cover-up could be life threatening if your vehicle breaks down somewhere out in the boonies on a sub-zero night with no help to be had. It would give a new meaning to "die hard."

The Borrowed Dress

When researching this one, I was quite surprised. Re-selling used products happens more than you think.

I know a few women who have actually bought party dresses, taped down the price tags on the garment, wore them, and then returned them to the store! They would make an excuse as to why they couldn't keep it, and in turn receive their refund and be on their merry way. What did the store do with the second hand dress? They placed it back on the rack as is!

This little trick is easy to check out. Sometimes your "new" dress smells of stale cigarette smoke. If you have friends or acquaintances employed at a store like this, just ask them. By the way, this devious act isn't just done with party dresses. Almost any item you can imagine is often "borrowed" from the store, only to be returned and then re-sold. A friend of mine told me about a family who bought all their kids new clothes, had their pictures taken in them, and then took the items back.

Who wants to take time purchasing a "new" television or computer only to find out that it doesn't work properly? Look for resealed packages or boxes. Furthermore, inspect clothes for makeup, spots or other flaws. However, it's difficult to detect certain used items. For example, I'm told that jewelry and books are difficult to spot if returned. I know this to be true since book stores are looking more and more like libraries.

More Or Less?

Buying in bulk is not always the best way to go. Let's look at detergent for instance. Compare the cost of one gallon to the quart and you may find that you would actually pay less for four quarts than the gallon size. Don't assume bigger means better when it comes to price.

In fact, at many fast food places or movie theaters, you have the choice of selecting a small, medium or large drink. Choose the small size, since the establishment's policy is to re-fill your cup as many times as you want!

Many times a store will have a "combination sale." A mop and bucket combo may be advertised as a "package." However, the same identical items are being sold at an individual price. The mop and bucket together may cost 6^{95}. Upon checking, the mop turns out to be 2^{50} and the bucket 2^{50}. Here, the shopper actually saves 1^{95} when purchasing the products singularly.

Don't forget to check out the ingredients of a product. Some of us think that name brands are better than generic or discount brands, especially for shampoos, lotions, or aspirin. Check the label! True, it takes a little extra effort, but the savings will be well worth it. Many times the ingredients of the contents are identical. Does it matter to you that the "discount" packaging is not as appealing as long as you are getting the same goods?

The New York Times

Saturday, November 12, 1994   *Sabra Chartrand*

Selling Homes: Is the Agent Getting Too Big A Cut?

People are paying real estate agents too much for selling their homes, the Consumer Federation of America says. ... ... Furthermore, many Americans pay the commission under the impression that the price is regulated or dictated by law, the survey found. 'For many years, one of the secrets of the real estate profession has been that consumers can negotiate commission,' said Stephen Brobeck, executive director of the federation. ...

Home Smarts

There are certain items that home buyers must check. Of course the number one item would be to make certain that you are paying a fair price. The reason home costs are not always fair is simple: *greed.*

Let's start with the seller who usually wants to get a general idea as to how much money the sale will bring. They will call a few real estate agents in order to obtain the value of their home. To simplify, let's say the market value (what the house will sell for if listed by a broker) is $100,000. The broker believes the house should sell <u>close</u> to that price. The process the broker uses to arrive at market value is fairly simple. Most brokers work for real estate companies listed with Multiple Listing Services (or <u>MLS</u>). By being a member, they are entitled to receive an <u>MLS</u> book, which lists all homes that have been sold in the past. It gives inside and outside descriptions of the home, as well as the original listed price, plus the final price at which it was sold. This way the broker is able to compare various homes that have sold in the same area. Then, by comparing "like" houses in similar neighborhoods, the sales rep gets a "handle" on approximately what the seller's home will bring on the market. These lists of homes are generally six months to a year old. This is called the "market value," not to be confused with <u>appraisal</u>. Market value is an educated guess that brokers make based solely on <u>past</u> sales of comparable houses in like neighborhoods.

Now here's where the house gets overpriced. Homeowners want the $100,000 for themselves; so the listing broker tells them that they can get $110,000 for the home. That means after the agent's commission, (anywhere between 5%-7%), the homeowner will be guaranteed their $100,000 plus in profit. Again, let's keep the arithmetic simple: $110,000 minus 5% commission comes to $104,500. So there. The seller can still list with the real estate agent and make over the $100,000 they were counting on. Therefore they list with an agent and sell. Right?

No, they don't always do that. Some sellers want it all, so they become FISBO's (For Sale By Owner). They want the whole pie or $110,000. They stick a sign in their front yard that reads "For Sale By Owner" and then they wait. Since most of them do not know how to sell, market, or advertise, they usually end up back with a real estate broker, though not necessarily the one who did the original market appraisal. They are too embarrassed. The greed factor failed. So, the sales agent takes over. They list or ask somewhere in the neighborhood of $110,000 as planned. This price is, of course, around $10,000 too high. Sometimes the agent will get the $110,000. You know, they work on the premise of whatever the market will bear. That would be you the buyer doing the bearing. But most of the time the price will be closer to the actual value, or $100,000. In the previous example, this will give the seller $100,000 minus 5%, or $95,000. This would be fair because the agent has earned his commission. But what do you as the buyer then have?

As the purchaser of a home you shouldn't overpay. Avoid at all costs paying a commission for a real estate agent. That's the seller's responsibility. Therefore, you must offer a lower price than the asking price. Don't be afraid that you're going to hurt someone's feelings. Let the seller's agent worry about that. Offer what other homes in the area sell for. Seek out an agent you trust if you feel you need help. Ask a friend or relative about the real estate firm they dealt with, and if they were satisfied. Most of the time you will save a great deal of money. Of course to accomplish all of this price negotiating, you must not "fall in love" with the house that's for sale or you'll be a push-over. Do you think you can be smart and buy smart? I do. I've never paid full price for any piece of real estate I've ever purchased, and I've bought many.

PART II:

Service Tricks

Another X-Ray

X-rays. Do we need them? And who owns them?

You can go to one doctor one day and have an x-ray taken and the very next day visit another doctor and they will want to take another one! Why? Money. To this day I've not the foggiest idea as to how much profit there is in taking x-rays, but due to the constant repeating and duplicating of them, it must be huge.

Other than the cost factor, you may want to take a look at the long term health risk. For example, health care providers advise patients that x-rays are not dangerous. If this is the case, then why do technicians place leaded shields over you and then go hideout behind a lead wall?

Since you don't sign a copyright agreement, let's face it, x-rays are *yours* and paid for by you. Even when your insurance company pays, it's still on your behalf. You pay the insurance premiums.

Why do some doctors want to charge you again for the reproduction of your x-ray when you are terminating your relationship with them? Bingo! It's money. More for them, less for you. Ownership, unless stated by some sort of nutty contract between you and the medical provider, should be yours. Next time you change doctors, remind them that you already paid for your x-rays once. They should waive any "reproduction" costs.

IN THE NEWS   **THE WALL STREET JOURNAL.**

Tuesday, August 3, 1999   *Staff Reporter*

FTC Charges 25 Companies With Fraud In Travel Deals

The Federal Trade Commission, along with other federal and state authorities, charged 25 companies with fraud for misleading consumers about vacation packages, FTC officials said. ...

Vacation Nightmares

When planning your vacation, make sure you do a thorough investigation on all your accommodations. I always chuckle when I think of some of the fishing trips I took. What I expected was not always what I got.

On one of my fishing trips, I noticed there were no fish cleaning facilities. *Hello!* This is supposed to be a "fishing resort!" It appeared that the fish cleaning station had rotted away over time, so naturally my cabin became the next best substitute. The smell was awful! I drove twenty miles to the nearest town for live bait since the bait shop had also been phased out, much like the fish station.

Then, after a long day of fishing, I found myself sitting inside a "screened" porch at night with no screens. There were other disappointments, believe me...too many to list here. Bottom line: What I expected was not what I got. Enough time has passed, however, that it now brings a chuckle out of me when I tell the tale.

Yet there are three important factors to give serious thought to:

1. Where will you be sleeping;

2. How far will you be from the nearest town; and lastly, but maybe the most important,

3. What's in the lake other than rocks and logs?

Fishing magazines and brochures typically display groups of people holding up a long stringer of large fish. Look down at their boots. Your first clue to the "come-on" is the age of the picture. Sometimes the people are wearing 1930's hightop shoes and hats that don't even exist anymore! When have you last seen someone wearing a campaign hat with a strap under his chin? More than likely, the lake has been fished out for over half a century.

Your living quarters are referred to as "sleeping accommodations" because in order to remain in them, you have to be asleep. My room had a bed with broken springs. Now I could wake up with a backache and not worry about getting one while fishing. And the plumbing in the cabin was out of order. Everyone had to use public facilities up the road by the main lodge.

Remember I mentioned that it would be a good idea to know how far you are away from town? It's a good idea. If for some crazy reason you decide to stay, you need a place to find food, bait, and finally a place to entertain yourself until you're too tired to stay awake so you can flop down back at the lake and fall asleep. Just make darn sure you get some references about your holiday choice other than an old or new brochure.

A few years back I decided I would return to Europe and do some sightseeing while conducting business. I sent away for information about a bus tour company. Here's what I found out.

The touring company had a brochure and elaborate travel magazine that explained in detail about the comfort of their busses, or "luxurious coaches," as they referred to them: large windows, over-stuffed seats, great intercom systems, and of course restroom facilities. Yes, the bus "had them all." Except that the restroom couldn't be used. Why? Because France, Germany, and Italy don't have the pumping facilities to accommodate the cleaning of waste tanks on a bus. At this point, large windows and a loud intercom really came in handy. We could not only see the sights as we drove down the roads, but we could also look and listen for the tour guide to inform us *when* we were going to stop. Everyone caught on quickly how to pace themselves. Being a Hoosier, I am well aware of pace cars at the Indianapolis 500. Now I became keenly aware how to "pace" while on a touring bus in Europe.

A tip for honeymooners: Sometimes you'll get brochures with pictures of sunsets from a room with ocean views. When you arrive, your room has the view of another building or a parking lot. Don't believe everything you see in the brochure! Make sure that your reservation is for the room you are counting on—the one with the picturesque view.

A travel agency once booked a deep sea fishing trip for me at a resort in Key West. There were no boats or captains available! I ended up having to go down to the docks myself to attempt to locate an outfit. Once I found a captain, it turned out he didn't have a "bait boy." (For those not familiar with fishing, the bait boy is the one who rigs your rods and the captain is the one who pilots the yacht.) The captain had hired a kid from town who knew next to nothing about deep sea fishing. So when my partner finally caught a sailfish, he didn't have to decide whether to keep or release it. The "bait boy" knocked it off the line with a grappling hook. You can avoid this type of fiasco by carefully checking every detail out! Before you finalize the purchase of your "package" from a travel agency, get the name of your captain, and description of the boat. Make a phone call to him or her before finalizing your plans. My trip was a money-looser.

Since I've been writing about vacations, I might as well throw in transportation. The word "limousine" can be very confusing. When most of us think of a limousine, we visualize a stretch limo, what we see with movie stars, dignitaries, wedding parties, and prom dates. However, some limo companies (and they use the word "limo") have another view. A limo can be a four door sedan, an automobile that most of us consider a full size car. We really don't think of a limo as a taxi painted solid without a meter. If you think that you are getting a deal when you are quoted a price for a limo, once again, you'll have to ask about the type of vehicle they are sending to pick you up. Don't be shy. It's always better to be safe than sorry.

A final tip. When booking a flight for a vacation anywhere, make certain you check out several airlines. You can even do this on the internet, if you have access. Some flights are non-stop, others have lay-overs. There's also a big difference in fares during the week as compared to the weekends. Several web-sites offer discounted fares so you can let your computer do the checking for you. Many airlines overbook reservations because of aborted flights, canceled tickets, etc. If you want to guarantee yourself a seat when scheduled, you'd better arrive early at the airport. Often when overbooked, an airline representative will offer you free overnight accommodations plus $500 and a ticket on another flight if you give up your seat. It's a good deal if you aren't in a hurry to get to your original destination on schedule.

If it's an important flight for you, one that you must catch at a definite time, then book first-class. It costs more, but your reservation guarantee is about 99%. Also, you may opt to take a later flight—the one they call the "red eye." These flights are more inconvenient to most of our schedules, but they also have many empty seats. "Red eyes" are scheduled either very late at night or very early in the morning.

Even if you have previously scheduled your hotel or motel reservation, you may be surprised when you arrive. Once, when traveling with my youngest son, I made sure well in advance that I had received a guarantee from the motel that my room would be waiting. But upon arrival, there were people sitting all about in the lobby waiting for their room. I showed the desk clerk my confirmation and she informed me that there were no rooms available. It seems that many of the guests decided to stay a couple of nights longer. They couldn't be thrown out. Only after a long hassle was I able to secure a room for my son and myself.

A good way to avoid being "left out in the cold" is to book a room with a large motel chain, one that has multiple locations close to your destination. This way, if one facility is full they will be able to accommodate you in a nearby one. Of course, in the event of an emergency, such as a snowstorm or flood, it's "any port in the storm." You may end up sleeping in the lobby.

When you're in these situations, you are at the mercy of the representatives in charge. If you stay relatively calm, but firm, you can usually be accommodated. Remember, "The squeaky wheel gets the oil?" Well here's the other half of that old adage: "If the wheel squeaks too much, it gets the ax!" You know, when someone makes you so angry that you don't care about their needs anymore and you lose "your cool?" Keep your cool, and chances are you'll get what you need.

If diplomacy is not your cup of tea, then you might want to have an alternate plan in case this one fails.

Who's Taking Who
For A Ride?

Having a rental car waiting for you when you arrive at your business or vacation destination can be accomplished quite easily if you take the proper precautions. This is necessary because, at times, rental agencies don't get their vehicles returned to them on time due to layovers or extended stays.

First, rent a model that is in <u>least</u> demand. For example, most people want a small or medium-sized vehicle. This usually saves a couple of dollars. However, if it's not there when you are, it for sure won't save you any grief. *Second,* make certain you are dealing with a well-known national rental agency. Their vehicles are more likely to be available since they have a bigger inventory.

The best and quickest way to reserve a rental car is by using a credit card, that way you have an instant record of proof. You can also decide if you will need the insurance they offer. If you own your own vehicle, check with your insurance agent to see if your coverage transfers to the rental. Most of the time liability coverage will transfer; however, you may need to purchase the rental agency's physical damage coverage under two circumstances. First, if you don't carry physical damage insurance on your own vehicle through your personal auto policy. Or second, if your insurance policy says that the physical damage does not transfer to the rental. If you should have to purchase the physical damage coverage through the rental agency, it will cost between fourteen and twenty dollars extra per day. This extra cost will vary with different rental agencies.

Another option you have is to check in the newspapers or with various rental agencies themselves. Many times they are looking for a driver to take one of their vehicles to a designated place. If you're fortunate enough, you not only have a free car, but they will also pay you for driving it.

Since most rental leasing forms are long and detailed, it would not be wise to make a generalization on insurance coverages and responsibilities. If you want to be filled in on all items, I suggest you request a blank agreement from the rental agency you plan on doing business with before you actually sign the lease.

IN THE NEWS   𝕿𝖍𝖊 𝕹𝖊𝖜 𝖄𝖔𝖗𝖐 𝕿𝖎𝖒𝖊𝖘

July 14, 1994

Chain to Pay $250,000 in Bait-and-Switch Case

Nationwide Computers and Electronics has agreed to pay the state $250,000 to settle charges that it used bait-and-switch advertising and other deceptive sales practices, the state's Division of Consumer Affairs announced yesterday. ...

The Ol' Switch 'N Bait

"Bait and switch" is an old trick, but it rests in a gray area today. For instance, I previously told you about vacation brochures that are not up to date. The photo looks different from the actual accommodation. If asked, these salespeople would explain that they were not trying to deceive you, but were only showing you what they *do have* at an *additional cost.* Let's look at a few others.

1. The <u>newspaper</u> <u>advertisement</u> for a ten cubic foot freezer which is on sale. The ad shows a photo of a freezer that is ten cubic feet in capacity. However, when the customer arrives at the store, there are only two freezers on display next to each other—a ten cubic foot freezer and a seven cubic foot freezer. The sale price in the newspaper advertisement is put on the smaller freezer, while the price tag on the larger freezer cost much more. Conclusion? The ad "baited" the customer into the store thinking there was an exceptional buy, but then switched the item advertised in the sale flyer.

2. The <u>car</u> <u>salesman</u> is showing you a car <u>on</u>

display with greater horsepower, let's say a V-8 compared to a V-6 engine. You believe that you are purchasing the same car he is showing you. Wrong. The one you are buying has the smaller engine. However, the price quoted on the show-room model remains the same when it comes time to pay for the one you picked out on the lot. Of course, it doesn't have to be the engine size that is being changed. In the bait and switch it can be anything from A to Z.

3. The car floor mats you see in the show-room model. Not the standard rubber or vinyl ones, but the luxurious carpeted ones. You don't ask about the floor mats because you take it for granted that they are included in the vehicle you are buying. They are, if you are willing to cough up an additional $200.

The total cost you can bear will depend upon how much you can lose, as well on how much more money the dishonest sales representative will make. Some losses are less than others. For instance, losing your car keys doesn't measure up to the loss of the entire car. However, follow this reasoning, if a woman was to have $10 in her wallet and someone took $5 away from her, the loss would be half her money. If the same woman had $100 in her purse and lost $50, her loss would also be half. Maybe this is the reason why so many millionaires jumped out of skyscraper windows during the Great Depression. They were still rich, but had lost more than half of what they owned.

Does the same logic apply to being cheated? Is there in your mind such a principle as: "It's okay to be taken for just a little?" Probably not. Any loss is in direct proportion to what you can bear. If in buying a home the contractor cheated on the amount of bushes to be planted in the yard, would you care? Even if it was one less? Put yourself in the following cases and think of the loss as your own.

4. <u>The</u> <u>infamous</u> <u>model</u> <u>home</u>. Years ago it was popular to have cross-stitched pictures hanging on the wall that read, "Home sweet home." Actually, today they should read: "Home switched home." Reason being is that many times a contractor's model house is <u>not</u> <u>a</u> <u>model</u> <u>at</u> <u>all</u>. If you carefully examine the carpeting, hardware, fixtures, lawn, etc., there's a good chance you won't get what you're looking at.

<u>Case</u> <u>1</u>: This is what a friend of mine found out when she moved into her newly-built home. The basement walls leaked since they weren't properly sealed from the outside foundation. Within a few months, the drywall tape from the cathedral ceiling loosened and pieces of drywall fell down. Some of the doors stuck. Electric wiring was hooked up improperly, causing the ceiling fan to work instead of the lights. Caulking around bathroom fixtures was poor, causing leaks. The backyard was pitched toward the house, causing rain water to run *toward* the house instead of *away* from it. As a result, the basement was wet. All of this can happen to you, if an unscrupulous builder is selling you "a home." Even if you have a good contractor, there's always the chance of poor tradesmen working for him. That means both you and he can be "in the dark" as to "cutting corners."

If you're like a lot of people who don't know about the building business, I suggest you hire an overseer to review and report on the work. He could be an architect. If this isn't possible, then you need to get recommendations from the Board of Realtors, the Chamber of Commerce, or any other professional organizations to which the contractor may have some association. Buying a home is too large of an investment for you to take a chance on.

Case 2: Here's another story. A contractor had a man who worked for him for over twenty years. This man was not only an excellent carpenter, but he was also a "jack of all trades." He knew all about plumbing, bricklaying, electric and roofing—everything. He was the contractor's "general foreman." Since he was so loyal, his boss decided that the next house he built, he would give all the profits to his general foreman. He gave him full authority to run the job of building a house. He also informed him that cost was not a priority.

The foreman was pleased. He could see that if he used his head, he stood to make quite a profit for himself. Therefore he cheated on the materials being used to build the new home. Rather than the required sixteen inch centers on the framing, he made them eighteen inch centers, thereby saving on lumber costs. For the concrete, he used more sand and less cement. Cheaper grade shingles were used on the roof and inferior floors were put in place. In fact, wherever he could fudge and skimp on materials, he did. Since he didn't care about the quality of the work, the job was completed much sooner than usual. This way he could cut labor costs.

Finally, when everything was finished, he went to the contractor and told him it was ready to be occupied. The house could be sold. The contractor told him that because of his honesty and hard work, the house was never built to be sold. Instead, it was his gift to his most loyal and dedicated employee. The boss shook his hand and wished him much happiness in his new home!

So, first. Have the contractor put everything in writing!

Second. Read the contract's fine print. Make certain you are getting what you expected.

Third. Have a lawyer read your contract.

Paper Capers

Coupons aren't always what they're cracked up to be. Take a supermarket coupon discounting ice cream by $1^{00} per carton. When you read the small print, it may read "selected varieties only." This means that you pay full price on all favorite flavors, while the coupon only applies to *less popular* flavors. The coupon may even apply to a less popular *brand*.

Sales flyers and ads don't always tell the full story either. A flyer may show a complete computer package, including the main processing unit, monitor and keyboard. However, the only item on sale is the main processing unit. Upon reading the fine print, you discover the monitor and keyboard are not included. Bargains aren't always what they seem to be.

My mother was a push-over for those flyers or ads in various magazines, especially around the holidays. Here's where a picture is <u>not</u> worth a thousand words. One Christmas she ran across an ad that advertised one hundred Christmas ornaments for only $10! The picture showed beautiful, large ornaments. When they arrived they were about one inch high. An examination of the fine print would have revealed that the photo was not to scale.

Many times a sale ad will have the correct size, but incorrect count. The advertising will correctly read "two for one." Yet the picture will display three or more of the articles on sale. Subliminally it makes us think that we will receive more than what is being advertised. It's best to read the small print on *any* sale item. For example, a product is on sale for $6⁰⁰. When reading the very small print, you discover that the six dollar sales price is "after the manufacturer's rebate of fifty cents." The present price is actually $6⁵⁰, and yet once you buy a postage stamp and envelope to send in for the rebate, you've not saved any money at all!

Same with many discounts. Do you really get 25%, 40%, or 50% off? Not usually. In many cases, you think the sales price to be an excellent deal, considering that the original price of an item was so much higher. Take a piece of furniture that shows the original price as $950. It's on sale for $650. Is this deal actually as good as it seems? Not usually. The item never sold at $950, and was probably always ticketed somewhere around $650. It doesn't take a genius to figure out that the price can be whatever the store places on it. However, if an item always sold at a competitive market price of $650, then you are not getting any discount! To receive a 50% discount on an item that has a $650 value, you'd pay $325. Inflating prices to more than an item is worth, then discounting to actual price is another way of baiting. Here's another example: A pack of gum normally costs 25¢. So if it's priced at 50¢, then discounted 50%, nothing's changed. The gum is still selling for 25¢.

One more trick. A shoe store advertises a certain style on sale. When you arrive at the store, you find that a white pair is only on sale. You want the black ones in stock; however, they are not on sale. Many stores do this. They believe that once they get you in, you will walk out happy, and settle for the over-stocked color on your feet!

When looking for sales or shopping in general, always keep in mind what it is you are wanting to purchase and what you won't settle for, even if the price is very appealing. Many times we find ourselves buying items that end up never being used. As I've said, have buying goals!

Otherwise, those coupons, or baits, will have your money flying out of your pockets.

On Sale Or Sold OUT!

Grocery stores always seem to have "sales." So make sure you check the sale out before you "check-out." In the dairy product section you see half gallons of milk on sale for $XX dollars. You grab a couple of them and maybe a dozen eggs while you're at it. At the check-out counter, you are told the milk is on sale only if your purchase comes to $25 or more. The clerk tells you that there's a small sign located "somewhere" in the dairy section. How many of us are looking for "small signs" in a supermarket? Now you must make a decision. Take the milk back or buy it. Most people make the purchase. Mark one up for the grocery store.

Want to hear a better one? Okay, you're with a friend and she's doing her shopping on a

Wednesday. In the meat section, several varieties of roasts are on sale. She buys a few. You tell her you will have to come back on Friday since that's the day you get paid. On your return, you also pick up some roasts, because of the "sale." Oops! When checking out, the clerk informs you that meat is only on sale Monday through Thursdays. Make your choice. Your cart is full, the line behind you is backed up. You go ahead and check out. Round two for the supermarket!

Final round and knockout. Next shopping trip you're in the cereal section. On grabbing a box of cereal you discover that the box is slightly crushed. Why buy a damaged box? You return the damaged one, then reach way to the back and pull another one out. This box is the same size and brand as the one you just replaced but with one small difference: on the front is a coupon for 50¢ off at the check-out counter. This is the newly delivered cereal. Hello! If you buy

THIS box, you save money. [By mistake, round three goes to you.]

Since I took you to the check-out counter, and it's the last place you'll visit while at the supermarket, remember this: <u>watch</u> <u>the</u> <u>scanner</u>! Sometimes they're programmed with incorrect pricing of certain items. Scanners have even been known to malfunction, causing an item to be rung up twice. Or has it ever crossed your mind that a dishonest cashier could scan an item twice, later correct the mistake, and then keep the "extra" for her wallet? The answer to this one is simple: watch your totals as they're scanned. If you see an error, bring it to the cashier's attention immediately.

In order to take advantage of all the tricks going on in supermarkets, you'll have to do more than just check expiration dates on products that have been placed at the bottom or in back of the pile. Keep your eyes open!

THE WALL STREET JOURNAL.

Thursday, November 5, 1998

IBP Inc.: Possibly Contaminated Beef is Recalled from Customers

IBP Inc. said it is attempting to recall all 278 tons of ground beef produced at its Dakota City, Neb., processing plant on Oct. 22. The nation's largest beef processor said a sample of the meat had been found to 'possibly contain' the potentially dangerous bacterium known as E. coli 0157:H7. IBP, based in Dakota City, said it is contacting 71 grocery stores, food-service customers and other customers in 33 states that bought the meat, and is asking them to return the product. ...

This May Grind You

A couple of years ago, there was a documentary on television about grocery stores that took ground beef beginning to age and mixed it with fresh meat. Then they repackaged it and placed it back with other meat items. Whoever started doing this figured they had a good idea. Someone's always trying to build a better mousetrap. With this meat "mixing and fixing" episode, they did.

Why mix fresh ground beef with old beef at all? Save time and money. Take the old expiration date off the old meat, re-wrap, and slap a new expiration date on the package. If it smells good, it sells good.

This next trick smells from the start! Let's say a grocery store has a brand named item on sale. When they run out of that particular brand named item, is the sale over? No, it's not. If a name brand sugar is sold out, this doesn't mean there's not room to still sweeten a sale. All the market has to do is conveniently forget to pull the advertisement and continue to fill orders with lower cost sugar. This is more than a "sweet" deal for the grocery store, since they'll make profits. You'd better know where you are buying your food, or know an insider to make sure you are getting what you paid for. If you're lucky enough to live near one, you'll go to a store that moves a lot of meat and turns over their products quickly, so that you'll always be assured of freshness.

Who's Goin' Fishing?

When booking a guide for your next fishing trip, you may have a few of these same bad experiences I'm about to share with you, unless you ask questions before you finalize your plans.

Here are a few stories for you to consider.

Unless you're an exceptional talent and have your own yacht, you will need a guide who also has experience as captain for deep sea fishing excursions in search of sailfish. You need someone who has an idea of where they are and the means to get the fish. It's when the fishing begins that you should be the most careful.

On my first sailfish trip, the captain never did take our party out to where the creatures were to be found. Instead, he ran us out to old tuna beds. The rest of the day we fished for tuna that he could sell to his local restaurants. Pretty clever, eh? After all, what were a couple of guys staying in a motel going to do with tuna? We were fishing on board a yacht for a captain who had an agreement with some local cronies! Since this little scheme is common, here's how to avoid it.

When *you* charter *your* deep sea fishing excursion, tell the captain of the boat that if *you* happen to catch tuna or any fish other than the sailfish, *you* are going to have him release it. It's your right to decide what to do with fish, since the captain and his boat are <u>hired</u> <u>for</u> <u>your</u> <u>fishing</u> <u>pleasure</u>. Once he understands your feelings about paying him to fish for his profits, he is more than likely to take you out to the gulf stream where <u>you</u> need to be in order to catch sailfish.

Maybe you don't like saltwater fishing, since your sport is freshwater fishing. Maybe your "dream" is to catch that big trophy bass, muskie or pike. If you're fishing a big lake that you're not familiar with, chances of catching "the big one" are greater if you hire a guide. He will provide you with his services, boat, fishing tackle, and knowledge— if he's a good one. However, here's how the trip can go sour. Most professional guides enter fishing tournaments for money and prizes. In order to win a tournament they have to keep improving their knowledge and skill about how to find and catch fish. Therefore, they will attempt to fish with you on your "guided" trip for practice and to bone up. Their focus is not on you, but instead on trying out different lures on y<u>our</u> rod. They are practicing for themselves.

Tip 1: Most bass boats used by guides are set up for only two people, and equipped with seats raised approximately three feet high from the bottom of the boat. This gives the occupant more freedom to cast and retrieve their lures while fishing. If you don't ask about the seating arrangements of the boat, one of you may find yourself standing all day, or sitting on one of the rod compartments while trying to fish.

Tip 2: If you're not taking your own fishing tackle, make sure the guide has a good rod and reel for you to use. It's a given that he won't let you use his. However, he should provide you with one that will not give you problems, like "back-lash" every time you cast.

Guides themselves can be a problem. I have experienced everything from one who got lost to one who fell out of his own boat. Fishing in Texas one year, I was accompanied by an experienced guide who was featured in one of the popular bass fishing magazines. Returning to the lodge after a long day of fishing, I asked her if I could help her with anything, like carrying the tackle boxes, or the fish, or help her dock the boat. She snapped, "No!" I guess she took my offer as chauvinistic, or maybe she was just doing her job. Anyway, I went up to the lodge and after awhile I began wondering where she was. I returned to the boat dock to find her standing on the pier, soaked from her neck down. I asked her what happened. She told me that she had fallen off the stern of the boat while tying it down. Oh well, at least she didn't get us lost in the Canadian wilderness, like one male guide did when I was fishing there.

So, if you are planning a trip, remember, make sure it's one that gives you a good chance of getting a prize catch. Check out the guide through his or her professional memberships.

Ask questions before you hire the guide, questions about equipment, seating arrangements, and the time you'll spend on the lake or ocean. After all, your kidneys will need a break too! Don't believe that I'm overemphasizing the problems which can arise. I was once with a female guide and the only "can" I saw all day was the one she used to relieve herself. Let's face it, some folks don't like to "go" over the side of a rocking boat with everyone watching.

PART III:

Trickier Tricks

Read The Small Print

Now that I have described some of the more common cons, let's turn to those "tricks" which are a little more clever.

Many times the whole can be understood by looking at the part. For example, while driving down the highway you spot a neon sign that reads, "E_T HERE." Your mind connects the burned out "A" and completes the message for you, "EAT HERE." We are reminded that as creatures of habit that we sometimes view things as we best remember them. I believe that is how merchants take advantage of you by selling products. They reduce *the measurement in terms of the quantity of product sold.*

Customers are used to purchasing products by the pound. When you visit the butcher, and look at meat prices. You find that luncheon meats, beef cuts, and other items are sold by the pound—ham: $1^{90}. However, today with a little imagination, the retailer may have a sign that reads: ham, 1^{95}, and in small print, per <u>half</u> pound. Yet our thinking process is still "per pound." That's exactly what the grocer <u>wants</u> us to think. That's the reason for the small print.

To avoid getting taken on these *slight of sign* tricks, you are going to have to pay close attention to what you are looking at. If it's ham you are buying, don't just assume that because other luncheon meats have signs that read per pound that ham is sold by the pound. If there's no sign on the meat you are purchasing, ASK! Otherwise, you will be surprised at the checkout counter. That's if you're paying attention.

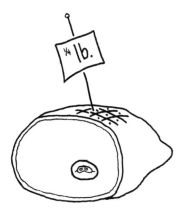

Small print works great for other businesses too. Take the carpet store for example. Most everyone who's had the opportunity to purchase carpet knows that it is sold by the <u>square yard</u>. Right? Wrong. Next time you're shopping for carpet, you'll find that many places are now advertising by the <u>square foot</u>. Big difference in price. You can look for "the measurement" in their advertisements, store signs, and most importantly on the sales contract before you sign it.

Carpet scams are an easy one to "duck" if you have your room size written down. Say the room you are planning to carpet is ten feet by twelve feet. That's one hundred and twenty square feet. When you are talking to the carpet salesperson, keep your buying goal in mind—that is, how much will it cost to cover a room with one hundred and twenty square feet. Don't let the carpet salesperson talk to you in *their* terms, which could be square <u>inches</u>. Big difference!

Some sales reps like to talk over the buyer's

head or keep them in the dark. That way they get you thinking you're stupid if you ask too many questions. Personally, I would rather they think I'm stupid than a pushover. Pushovers lose money with "fast-talking" salespeople!

IN THE NEWS   𝕿𝖍𝖊 𝕹𝖊𝖜 𝖄𝖔𝖗𝖐 𝕿𝖎𝖒𝖊𝖘

February 1, 1998   *Jay Romano*

New Jersey Licensing Inspectors

... But the vast majority of those who conduct home inspections are themselves unlicensed because most states, New York and Connecticut included, have no requirement for the licensing of home inspectors. ...

... 'Until this law was passed, anybody with a ruler and a flashlight could say they were a professional home inspector,' said Assemblyman Anthony Impreveduto, Democrat of Secaucus, sponsor of the law. 'Now they're going to have to prove it first.' ...

Inspector Dependent

Home inspectors are individuals who, for a fee, inspect the house you are planning to purchase before the deal is finalized. People providing these inspection services are usually independent businesses. That is, they are not usually employees of the real estate firm selling the house.

Most home purchase agreements completed by any real estate broker have a clause that covers independent inspections. They provide for basically two things: one, giving the buyer a choice to accept or reject hiring an independent inspector; and second, holding all real estate brokers involved in the transaction "harmless," that is, they are absolved of any liability relating to any defect or deficiency found on the property. This means as the buyer you're on your own! For example, if the roof is in bad shape, or ready to cave in, it's your "baby."

Here's what to look out for. Even if you *do* decide to hire an independent house inspector, make certain that he is just that! INDEPENDENT. Otherwise you may be hiring one *who works for the broker!* If this is the case, the inspector may not be so quick to point out defects to you. After all, they make their money on doing inspections. There's always the chance that if they find too many problems (one's that will kill or slow down the deal, or cost the buyer more money), and report them, they may not be recommended by the real estate broker for future work.

Next, consider hiring one from out of town. That is, one with no vested interest with local brokers. Furthermore, there are many general contractors or architects who, for a fee, will take a look at the house. In addition, if you are getting a bank loan, bank officials might refer you to one of their own inspectors. After all, the bank has a financial interest if they are holding your mortgage note.

IN THE NEWS   **THE WALL STREET JOURNAL.**

| Tuesday, July 6, 1999 | *Lucette Lagnado*
Staff Reporter |

Columbia/HCA Healthcare Convictions May Bolster Case for Civil Settlement

... Friday's convictions in Tampa, Fla., of two Columbia/ HCA Healthcare Corp. managers could strengthen the hands of prosecutors pursuing Medicare fraud investigations in several cities and boost the leverage of the Justice Department in its settlement talks with the Nashville, Tenn., hospital chain. ...

Health "Care-Less"

Before you are released from a hospital or after you've been treated as an outpatient, hospitals expect you to sign many forms. Be certain to take time and read them in their entirety. Especially read them carefully if you have health insurance coverage.

All hospitals want to be guaranteed that they are going to get all of their money. They want all charges paid as stated. Here's the problem. Many times what the insurance company's policy allows to be paid on certain charges is in direct conflict with what the hospital expects to receive. For example, the hospital charges $X number of dollars for an anesthesiologist or a lab test. This amount can, and many times is, higher than what the insured patient is afforded under their HMO or hospital plan coverage.

The hospital will then attempt to have you sign a form that says: any charges which are not paid in full by your policy will be your responsibility. Not a good deal on your behalf!

First of all, the people in the billing department of the hospital will not put up much of a "fight" with the insurance company if they know they have you, "the little guy," to go after. See, they will try to get you in the middle of a big debate which today goes on between health care providers and insurance companies. In the meantime, they will "sic" their collection department on you. Do you want all that grief? Here's a suggestion to avoid having to sign the hospital's forms. Advise them that you gave them your health information before being admitted; however, if they need additional information, request they give you blank forms so you may seek advice from your insurance agent.

Sometimes I wonder why they call it *health* care. It seems at times it would be better labeled *money* care. When I've been a patient, someone always asks me about my hospital coverage, instead of my health.

Ũhe New York Times

Friday, November 19, 1999   *Leslie Eaton*

Penny-Stock Fraud Is Billion-Dollar Game

Most Americans may not know it, but there are really two Wall Streets.

One is the Wall Street of the New York Stock Exchange closing bell, of brash stockbrokers and hairtrigger traders, of big deals and big fortunes, of Microsoft and mutual funds.

But in the crooked alleys of Lower Manhattan flourishes another Wall Street. This is a world of low-priced stocks and high-priced dreams, of grimy offices and sham companies, of swindlers and touts who prey on average people trying to grab the brass ring in the greatest bull market in American history. ...

Piggin' Out!

A "churn" is a container in which butter is made out of milk or cream. The term "churning" is also used when a person selling securities (AKA stock broker or investment broker) takes his customers accounts and "turns them over" for his own benefit, not yours. For example, a broker convinces his client to buy certain stocks. Then he turns around and suggests they sell. The broker gets paid a commission when he buys the stock and also when he sells it. So, if you happen to conduct your business with some unscrupulous broker, there's a good chance that you'll decrease your chances of receiving higher returns on the securities you hold.

Let's pretend that your broker buys you some XYZ stock at $30 a share. He receives a commission of 3% for his services, or $9 per share. Since stock is usually purchased in blocks of 100 shares, you pay $3,000 for XYZ's stock. The broker's total commission then would be $90. Within a couple of months, or sometimes just a few days, he suggests you sell XYZ because the price has risen to $35 a share. You would then receive $3,500 (that's 100 shares X $35 per share). He gets his commissions for selling it. For simplicity, I use the same 3% commission, or in this case, $105 for him. As you can see, in a short period of time he has made $90 for buying and $105 for selling, or a total of $195 commission. On the other hand, your total profit is $305 ($500 profit from the sale of stock MINUS the broker's commissions of $195). Your return is approximately 10% and you took all the risk. After all, the stock could have gone down. That's not my argument however.

My biggest complaint is that if the stock was given a chance, it could have gone *up* to $40 or more a share if held for a longer period. You might say to yourself at this point: "Well, it could have gone down and I would have lost money." Now that's just what I'm getting at. An unethical broker knows your fears of losing money. Therefore, while you make or lose small amounts of money, the "wheeler dealer" broker continues to rake in handsome commissions.

To prove my point, most investors discuss a certain stock with their broker and it is bought with the understanding that it is a risky or solid (Blue Chip) stock. If it's blue chip then there's a feeling of confidence that the conservative stock will increase over time. You know as goods and services rise in cost, so will the stock of a financially solid company that provides them.

Churning a client's stock is illegal. However at times it is difficult to prove. Especially when done with relatively small accounts held by middle-income people. After all, that's what ***Dirty Little Tricks*** is all about, helping people who don't know the ins and outs of the business world.

Here's how to avoid having your account churned. When you first purchase a stock, set your goal. For example, if you buy at $30 a share, decide immediately what you will sell it at. If it's $40 a share, stick to it. Once you sell at $40, you have reached your goal. If later you see that it climbed to $50 a share, <u>don't</u> <u>whine</u>. You've made your profit! The stock market is unpredictable. It's a gamble, but you can give yourself the edge by having buying and selling goals.

Also, with the availability of the internet, one can seek and find an abundance of information. You can type in the keyword "stocks" and numerous menus appear right at your fingertips (i.e., overviews of stock, company analysis, recommendations, financials, charts, and others). A good broker is worth every bit of his or her commission. However, it makes it easier for both the honest broker and the client if the client is educated at least on the language and workings of the marketplace.

Once upon a time there was a pig. His name was Blue Chip. He would go to his feeding trough every day to eat his corn. Once he got his fill, he would go back to his cool mud puddle and lay down. For some reason, Blue Chip decided that he wanted more food. Then it became even more and more. Then one day he finally ate so much that he just blew up. It didn't matter, because had he survived he would have become very fat and would have been sold at the <u>market</u> to be slaughtered. My moral of the story is when dealing with the <u>bears</u> and the <u>bulls</u>, don't become a <u>pig</u>.

A Real No Account

Many people depend on their accountant to keep them informed about tax deductions or changing tax laws. The reputable accountant can and does provide a needed service for us. Now let's discuss the dishonest ones.

The accountant I am going to discuss with

you is one who is even a Certified Public Accountant (CPA). It's a difficult designation to obtain. The final tests are extremely tough I'm told. This accountant not only practices accounting, tax filing, and bank reconciliations, but he also dabbles in investments. Some accountants hold a "Series 6 license," or an investment brokers license that expands their services. Why not? They have the best inside information you could possibly ask for. They know your income and savings.

Therefore, if you happen to hire the wrong person or should I say a dishonest accountant, you are in serious financial trouble. They can get you investing in bad business deals. They can con you into purchasing anything from dry oil wells, or bankrupt building projects, to hairbrained investments that always turn out to be losers.

The "rats" do this for money. Your money. They take your hard earned cash and invest it where they know that the commission or "finder's fee" is large enough for them. These conmen are worse than the old "snake oil salesmen" who sold from their wagons years ago. At least the "snake oil" didn't ruin you financially. It only hurt your pride. You were duped. Both these sales reps are "flim-flammers." However, the "no account" will leave you broke and bankrupt when given a chance.

There are ways to avoid them. First, check out the credentials of the accountant you retain. Inquire about them with your State Licensing Board. This way you can become aware of any past license violations or pending charges against them. Ask around. Check their professional memberships. Get good references from their long term clients.

But most of all, avoid those "get rich quick" schemes they might describe. It's always best to have a scrutinizing eye when dealing with a person who has snake eyes for your wallet.

What's Miss_ng?

Service or gas stations normally sell three grades of gasoline: super-unleaded, unleaded and regular. Most of the time the station has a large reader board on their lot that displays the price of fuel. The difference in cost between the three grades is usually around 10¢. If the super-unleaded is $1.^{10} per gallon, then the regular and unleaded are 90¢ per gallon and $1.^{00} per gallon respectively. So what's the problem? Missing numbers on the reader board fool the customer. For example, the second series of numbers on regular gas is displayed as $1._0, giving the customer the impression that the station ran out of numbers. The customer would quite naturally assume that the price of regular is $1.^{00}. Is it? Be careful. More than a couple of times I have found that the number is missing intentionally. The second price or the $1.^{00} regular is actually $1.^{20} at the pump! It's 10¢ more than the super-unleaded. See! The missing number is not always what you think. Check the price on the pump itself to protect yourself against this dirty little scam.

Instead of paying an attendant, many gas stations are computerized so you can actually pay and collect your receipt at the pump. Therefore, another trick to look for is the automatic credit card print out. When you place your credit card in the designated slot at the pump, your card will be checked for validity and then you will receive instructions to begin fueling. Once you have pumped in the amount of gas desired, you either lift a stop lever or the pump automatically shuts off when the nozzle is returned to its holder. The final process is to receive your receipt.

Here's where you might be paying for something you didn't ask for if you press the instruction button too hastily. The machine flashes the message: "Receipt?" and the customer is given the choice of "Yes" or "No" or, "Do you want a car wash?" The first "Yes" or "No" displayed is actually asking if you would like to have your automobile washed. Because you're anticipating a receipt without paying attention, you press "Yes." Then when you don't receive your receipt, you hit the yes button again, and place it in your purse or pocket and you're on your way, without a wash! Later, when you check your receipt, you find out you purchased a car wash that you didn't receive! You pressed the button before the receipt display was presented. Most of us press buttons fast because the options displayed on the pump turn off so quickly. When we miss our chance, we end up begrudgingly standing in line to pay while waiting behind individuals purchasing and scratching off lottery tickets. They're probably trying to recoup some of the money they lost at the gas pump.

Here are a couple of other items worth mentioning on service station receipts. When you're finished filling your gas tank and the instruction once again displays: "Receipt?" "Yes" or "No" and you press yes and nothing comes out of the slot. Why? The attendants inform you that they are out of receipt paper? I don't think so. This happens all too often to be believable. Once in a while it's true, they may be out of paper. Sometimes the "out of paper scam" is to entice you into the building. I have pushed "yes" for the receipt and guess what? I actually received a piece of paper that read, "See attendant in store to receive your receipt." Now you know why I rightfully have their intentions under suspicion. Of course if it's a <u>food</u> center too, then we have the "opportunity" to buy candy, chips, milk or some other item we weren't planning on. But it gives the gas station a chance to sell over-priced groceries.

"Short Drawered"

In the armed forces there was a standing joke or prank played on new recruits referred to as "short sheeting." You would take their bunk bedding apart and then remake the bed by taking the sheet and folding it in half. The new recruit would then get stuck, or be unable to stretch his legs out when climbing into his bed. It was a standard joke in basic training.

It's no joke when you are "short drawered" by a furniture store that sells you a dresser with shallow drawers, especially when the store claims to sell quality goods. Stores looking to buy furniture from a manufacturer who cuts corners will stock these "short" goods. A standard drawer should be approximately two to three inches less than the depth of the cabinet. In other words, a dresser that measures <u>nineteen inches</u> deep will have drawers that are <u>sixteen inches</u> deep. A "short drawer" might only measure thirteen inches deep, inside a nineteen inch deep cabinet.

Some time ago, I went shopping for a new bedroom suit. I ended up buying a bed, dresser, and chest of drawers (or should I say short drawers?). Not until placing my socks and shirts in, did I realize that the drawers did not pull all the way out! Why? I found out that they were manufactured that way to save on material costs. Why didn't I realize this at the store? Well, the salesman was showing me the wood and style of the set. He even pulled the drawers part of the way out to demonstrate how smoothly they worked on their guides. I never even considered that a dresser could or would have "half drawers." After all, every bureau I ever owned had full drawers. To this day, every time I reach into my drawer for a pair of socks, I feel "short-drawered!"

Today, no one can purchase any furniture at the store where I was duped. They are no longer in business. There are, however, many other furniture stores still selling this way. Again, impulse buying did me in. Think things through, take your time, check your purchases out carefully or you too may just become "short drawered."

𝕮𝖍𝖊 𝕹𝖊𝖜 𝖄𝖔𝖗𝖐 𝕿𝖎𝖒𝖊𝖘

Sunday, August 4, 1996   *Michael Cooper*

'The Mechanic From Hell'

... It was a Saturday in March 1994 and Ms. Schnabel could not scare up an authorized Saab dealer, so she thumbed through the Yellow Pages in search of a mechanic and settled on a company listed as 'AAA Midtown,' of West 50th Street. They sent a tow truck right away.

Ms. Schnabel did not realize it then, but her car troubles were just beginning. ...

... Back in Vermont, her mechanic, her insurance company and her car dealer confirmed her nagging suspicions: she'd been had. Mr. Barnes had not replaced any parts, not the oil pan, not the axle, not the transmission. About the most he had done, they told her, was a little hammering on a rim. And the insurance company was not rushing to reimburse her $4,132.25. ...

SO: Who To Trust?

Can we depend on every mechanic or service representative to be honest with us?

NO.

One day my air conditioning stopped working in my car. (It seems as though the air always goes out during hot weather). I took my car to one of the local dealerships. They had one of their mechanics check it out. The final diagnosis was that I needed a new air conditioning unit. Cost was somewhere in the area of $300. I had to make my decision: "To be or _hot_ to be."

Since I didn't at the time have $300 to cough up, I did what a lot of us do. I started checking around. At the advice of a friend, I ended up taking my car to an air conditioning/radiator repair shop. After a fifteen minute check, I was told it was only a fuse. I paid the cashier two dollars and might add I never had another problem with the unit for the next three years before I finally traded the car in. Can you believe it? A two dollar item!

Things don't <u>always</u> end up this simple when taking your car to the garage. Some unscrupulous technician may just "clean up" the "bad" part and never replace it at all. Your car may have a problem and the mechanic just might inform you that you had a faulty whatever and all he will do is replace a fuse and "clean up" the supposedly bad part and charge you a handsome fee. When inquiring about the old part, you will be informed that it was thrown away. Are we stupid? Why would the garage keep a useless part? No, we're not stupid, so we should always inform the mechanic that before he does any work, we expect to have the used part <u>returned</u> to us.

When the heating and air conditioning service rep visits your home to check the system that's not working, he might start *"hmmming"* like a family doctor. You will then feel there are a variety of things wrong. Cracks in the unit, motor wiring, stuck rotors, and on and on. There are many conmen in the heating and air conditioning business, and that's why many towns and cities make them purchase a license and permit bond just to do business in the community. They don't always replace that "fuse"– they replace the entire furnace! You'd best get references from relatives, friends, or business acquaintances. Also, you may want to check with your local Chamber of Commerce organization. Don't depend on cost alone or you might end up with a "fly by night" outfit that takes you to the cleaners to the tune of a couple thousand dollars!

When you buy a set of new tires for your car or truck, check around for the best price. Make sure you ask the same questions to each and every tire shop: "Did you figure in balancing?" "New valve stems?" "Same size, no *blems* (small blemishes on the tires but still pass inspections)?" "Labor included?" etc. You covered it all. Right? Good! Then once you go to pick up your car, you won't be surprised that there's an additional $20 charge. "What's that charge for?" you ask. Simple. It's for disposing of your old tires. Yet they turn around and sell them as used tires or spares. Now you know why you see tires on ropes in the primate cages at the zoo. The only rope trick you'll see is one of your old tires swinging from the end of it, and now, you're the monkey! In the future, when you get your quote, ask them how much they will give you for your old rubber. If they laugh and say they're useless, here's your opportunity to tell them they can have them; however, you don't intend on paying them for their freebies.

Disposal charges can also be applied to your old car battery. Therefore, make sure that when you replace your battery with a new one, you don't get stuck with an extra charge here either.

It's important to you and your wallet that you stay informed. If you're like me, getting screwed over a little or a lot is an aggravation that is unwelcome. However, if it doesn't matter to you, then neither will the other tips in this book.

PART IV:

Trade Tricks

The Masked Tape

Since our insurance agency does business with various automobile repair shops, I've run into my share of bad ones. Let me tell you a "masking tape story."

One day I contracted a body and fender repair shop to paint my car. Besides choosing my desired color, I had only one additional request: I wanted them to remove the chrome before they painted, rather than mask it. It was understood that removing the chrome was going to cost more. The shop owner assured me the car would be ready on Monday—this gave him the entire weekend to complete the job. Since he knew I had a fishing trip planned over the weekend, it worked out fine for the both of us. But guess what! My trip was cancelled! I dropped by the shop on Saturday to see how things were coming along. Nobody was around, so I took a peek in the window. The chrome on my car was masked with tape!

When I returned on Monday to pick up the car, the owner told me that he was losing money on the job because it was difficult to get the screws out of the channel on the side strips of chrome. Not until I told him of my visit did he fess up and tell the truth. He actually planned on cheating me!

The only way you can avoid this scam is by getting "word of mouth" references or knowing who you are doing business with. If I hadn't accidentally checked, I would have been paying that additional $400 the body shop owner wanted for removing the chrome he didn't.

THE WALL STREET JOURNAL.

Wednesday, August 11, 1999   *Associated Press News Service*

Auto-Parts Suit Against State Farm Nears Trial

When Peggy Frey picked up her newly repaired Ford Mustang from the body shop recommended by her insurance company, she found the hood didn't fit and the headlights were loose.

Ms. Frey, of Indian Shores, Fla., spent the next year battling with State Farm Insurance Co., contending it forced the shop to use substandard replacement parts when repairing her car after an accident. ...

Knock It Off

Another trick to look out for is auto body repair shops using "knock-off" or "after market parts." It's also known that some insurance companies approve of them. Why? It means that insurance companies pay out less on vehicle damage repair claims.

What is a knock-off part? Here's an example. When Ford or General Motors manufactures a fender, for instance, you have an original part.

However, if that same fender is produced by another manufacturer to be used as a look-a-like or replacement part, then it's referred to as a *knock-off* or *after market part.*

Many times it's difficult to tell the difference but there is <u>definitely</u> a difference. For instance, an original bumper may be stronger in damage resistance than its look-a-like counterpart. When the vehicle is in an accident, the after market bumper will not give the same protection against further damage caused by a collision. Weaker bumpers cause more damage to a grill and fenders. Also, if the same quality of steel is not used in the production of a knock off fender as was in the original, then the fender may rust out faster.

If the customer <u>knows</u> that they are getting parts of their damaged car replaced with after market parts, that's one thing. However, if they are kept in the dark and are made to believe their vehicle is being repaired with original parts, and this is not the case, then they are getting ripped off.

The best way to avoid being taken is, first, ask the insurance company adjuster if he is planning to authorize the body shop to use after market parts. Then, ask the body shop if they were told to use knock off parts. If you don't want look alike parts, tell them! Also, many times if you offer to pay the difference in cost to have an original part, the "shadier" body shops may come clean. After all, they will be thinking about making more money. Understand, it's a lot easier to camouflage a knock off fender then an emptied purse.

THE WALL STREET JOURNAL.

Friday, April 17, 1998

John J. Keller
Staff Reporter

It's Hard Not to Notice Phone Service Leaves A Lot To Be Desired

It seems that just about everyone has a nightmare tale about phone service these days. Maybe you have been 'slammed,' and found yourself receiving bills from a phone company you didn't choose, or 'crammed,' and paying for services you didn't order. Or maybe you have had to wait weeks to have a new line installed, or had your carrier's calling card rejected by a competitor's pay phone, or have found yourself punching a long string of digits to access your service. And perhaps, for all that, you're paying more. ...

"Phonies"

There are always better "calling packages" being introduced by cellular phone companies. Make sure you take advantage of the discounts offered. All cellular carriers are in competition to acquire new customers. If they're not giving away phones themselves they are at least vigorously competing on the cost of air time. For example, companies are sending out all sorts of direct mail explaining their new technology—such as clearer reception, longer battery life, etc. They offer more calling time for less cost; in other words, better calling packages. It seems more effort is spent on securing new customers. The same enthusiasm is not necessarily shown to the long-standing customer. Cellular companies aren't so quick to offer old, faithful customers better deals, unless the customer asks.

Three hundred minutes for $99 a month was the best the cellular company offered at the time I signed with them; shortly after I signed, however, they came out with a 700 minute package for only $69 a month. Obviously a better deal! I would not have found out about the new offer if I hadn't checked around with a couple of my colleagues at the office. Only after calling one of the service representatives was I asked if I would like to be converted to the new plan. Did I want to have more than double the calling time for two-thirds the price? Duh! Then I asked my cellular phone representative why the <u>customer</u> had to call in order to receive the company's best plan. Why didn't the <u>company</u> automatically give their customers the best plan? I was informed that she didn't know. She only worked there. Since so many of us have car phones, you would be surprised to find out that there just might be a better plan out there. Call and find out. It could save you quite a bit of money.

Trying to get through and talk to a warm-blooded human being at any company can prove a nightmare. Why do they make it so difficult to converse with someone directly instead of a machine or a "phone tree"? To cut costs, of course, and to avoid the customer complaints about their tricky techniques.

For example, screening calls can be such an elaborate system that after pressing numerous buttons in order to talk to an individual you need, you are finally worn out and hang up. Then you try again. After a while, out of exasperation, you'll leave a message with almost anyone. This, at times, will be useless, for the simple reason the message will be left with the wrong person, or even if the person it's left with is the right person, they often choose not to return your call.

Sometimes it's not a person you get, but a recording about the company's products or services. Actually, you don't need a message about their services, for when you started pressing buttons you discovered that service was not one of their major concerns. They may as well have you listen to music. They do! And all of this is supposed to save time and cut costs? How can the customer save any time when they never make contact? The customer keeps calling and the company keeps playing, "How are things in Glaca-MOR-A!!" They can cut some costs because they don't need any individuals to answer the phones, but what all this is leading to is the saving of time. Which brings me to my main point: With more time you can produce more and make more money.

By making more money you can take more time to do the things you like. I guarantee you that out of the two, time is much, much more important than money. I don't believe you've ever heard a person on their death bed say, "I wish I had more money." Time is the most precious commodity we have on this earth. It can never be replaced. Furthermore, it never stops ticking away. That's why I talk about it here in **Dirty Little Tricks: How Salespeople Are Robbing You Blind.** Whenever you have a salesperson waste your time, they've done you a grave injustice. Phone tag is rude, and a perfect example of time lost.

Phone systems are not the only way you can be robbed out of your time. Many times people themselves will oblige you. So, when you finally *do* reach someone, always get their name and position. Write it down. Next time you need to talk to them <u>you</u> will be able to <u>save</u> <u>time</u>.

Speed Bumps

Most everyone knows what a speed bump is. For those of you who don't, I'll explain. It's a slight bump in the road that measures approximately three feet in width and two inches in height and extends from one edge of the road to the other edge. The reason for a designed road bump is to slow down traffic. Slowing down can be for various reasons: school zones, neighborhoods with main thoroughfares, toll roads and dangerous curves, just to name a few.

However, salespeople sometimes refer to anyone who has the ability to <u>slow</u> <u>down</u> <u>the</u> <u>selling</u> <u>process</u> as a "speed bump." A speed bump is an intermediary between an individual and the salesperson. They can be receptionists, secretaries, or assistants. If these people are pleasant, helpful, or understanding, they can be of tremendous help to you the consumer. But if they act like "gate guards," they can be hard to get along with or impossible to get information from. Most of the time, authority is given to them by the hierarchy to help businesses move smoothly.

However, "speed bumps" will rob you of time and give you undue grief. Most of the time, these powerhouses are enclosed behind glass windows. There's just a small opening through which you are allowed to talk. Their title is usually "receptionist." You find them in large numbers in professional offices. When aggravated, we call them "window witches." Since you will have to deal with these people, it's best to try to win them over to your side. That is, don't argue with them. This will be a "no win" situation. I say: "Kill them with kindness!" They are such an important part of the process that professional sales reps have been known to bring them flowers, candy and other small gifts just to make certain a relationship is formed. As I previously stated, most people are kind and helpful, but remember your time is precious.

Leases Or Fleeces?

Many of us choose to lease vehicles rather than purchase them. This can be a good alternative, but check with your accountant. Making the deal could be a bad bargain if you're not careful to cover all the agreements in the contract you will be asked to sign. What I'm saying is that there is much more to signing a lease than coming to an agreement on monthly or annual costs. You must also consider what all is included in the lease: such as who's responsible for the insurance coverage, or what would be the difference between normal "wear and tear" versus vehicle damage, which is <u>your</u> responsibility. For instance, paint chips caused by everyday road gravel is accepted, however, a large dent in the hood caused by hail would be your responsibility to repair before the vehicle is turned in at the end of the lease. Also, you need to find out how many miles per year you are allowed to drive, what the dealer will allow as a trade-in at the end of the lease, or what the dealer will outright sell you the leased vehicle for if you decide to purchase it at lease end.

Let's assume that you are presently leasing your vehicle and that the lease period is coming up in a couple of weeks. The dealership where you signed the contract advises you that everything remains the same—same car, same features, same terms. Do you believe them? I don't. I leased a car some time ago and was told upon renewal of the lease that everything was "same-

same." You know, exactly as my previous lease. When I read the fine print I discovered I was getting 5,000 miles per year <u>less</u> <u>mileage</u> than before. Plus, I was going to pay an additional 5¢ more than I was previously charged for each mile I drove over the allocated mileage. Could all this have been avoided if I had done business with someone I knew well? No. I knew this dealer well.

My advice is clear. Read the contract with a critical eye. Save yourself time and money by asking for an advance copy of the new lease. Take it with you before you sign on the dotted line. Get away from the lessor and study the lease so that you can understand everything "promised." I did.

What Size Are Your Feet?

Even if you don't give two hoots about mathematics, it will serve you well to know the difference in measurements when purchasing certain items. As you probably know, 10 feet by 10 feet equals 100 square feet of floor space. If you were to cube the square feet you would have 10'X10'X10', or one thousand cubic feet. So what? Here's what.

If you are planning on purchasing a tool shed or a yard barn for your lawn equipment, you would be rather surprised if you thought 400 cubic feet would give you an abundance of storage space, unless you were figuring on filling the entire shed with concrete. You need to know the square feet because this will be the <u>useable floor space</u> you need to store your items, like mowers, gas cans, carts, or bicycles. So why the big deal?

Well, many television commercials and newspaper flyers advertise space in cubic feet, so you will believe that you are getting more for your money. You could say to yourself, "What's the difference? I would <u>see</u> the size of the barn or shed when I went to the store to check it out."

That would make sense as long as you didn't order it by mail. If you're not certain as to how much floor space is available in the shed, what you should do is use common sense. Ask the sales rep a question that both of you can relate to, such as: "How many bicycles or push lawn mowers will it store?" For example, when ordering by mail, state on the order form that you want to make sure you are buying a shed large enough to hold a lawnmower, two bicycles, a wheelbarrow, and a lawn cart. When it arrives you have it in writing what you expected. Make sure they have a return policy if you're not satisfied.

"Oily" Changes

There should be a simple and straightforward procedure to having the oil changed in your car. Is there? Nowadays, I find myself being sold all kinds of extra services provided by the individual changing my oil. How do you determine if these are necessary?

First, get an opinion from the dealership where you bought the car. A friend of mine was told that the fuel injection system in her car was dirty and in need of cleaning by "an oil change business." She phoned her dealership. The dealer explained that her vehicle had an internal check system which made the "check engine" light illuminate if there was a problem with the fuel injection system. She saved a considerable amount of money by declining the "oil change shop."

This is just one example of how you may be taken down the wrong path when it comes to bum advice. The way to avoid such situations is to <u>ask around</u>, seek out information from family and friends, and <u>read your maintenance manual</u>. Had my friend read it she would have known immediately that she was being scammed by an unscrupulous service rep who was only interested in making a couple of extra bucks in commission at her expense.

Oh yes, did you know that many mechanics are paid by commission? This gives the shady ones the opportunity to fleece you out of your hard earned money. Look out and be careful when you're doing business. Also ask for references from local organizations, like the Chamber of Commerce. Keep in mind that these people are not wearing an "I'm crooked!" name tag.

No Payment 'Til...

Are you aware of advertisements that claim "90 days same as cash," or "No payments until the year _ _ _ _"? What's wrong with this trick? It seems too good to be true, and if it seems too good to be true, then it probably is! What businesses don't advertise is that if you don't pay the full balance off at the <u>end of the ninety days</u>, you are then charged interest <u>back to the original date of purchase</u>!

The way some sales people conceal the rate

of interest they are charging should at least get them an unhonorable mention in the "Who's Who" of our business community. I'm referring to the offering of lower interest rates. Actually, they want you to re-finance your mortgage. This deal may not be all it's cracked up to be. Why? Even though you may receive a lower rate of interest than your current rate, there's always a gimmick to consider. Closing costs, or what they sometimes refer to as "discount points," will be such a large enough amount charged that when broken down and added to your monthly interest rate, it will exceed your present percent of interest. These offers are to take care of the greedy, not the needy. Watch out!

Saving money is easily accomplished in your choice of credit cards. Right off the bat, if you're paying an annual fee (you know...the twenty dollars or so you pay them so they can charge you interest?), ask them to remove it. That's right. *Just ask!* There are so many credit card companies vying for your business, they are usually quick to drop the annual fee when asked. After all, they are continuously lowering their rates, as well as adding a variety of "perks" such as insurance, product and service discounts, etc. They make plenty of money on credit card debt.

Many credit card companies also make a percentage on each of the products or services we purchase using our "plastic." For example, if you charge $100, the company giving the credit may receive $10 from the provider of the goods or service. This is another reason many credit card companies don't mind dropping an annual fee of twenty dollars or so. They can afford to give a little.

THE WALL STREET JOURNAL.

Friday, October 14, 1994   *Michael Selz*

Nightmare in Missouri: For Ted and Maryann Lapekas, Starting a Home-Based Business Almost Destroyed Their Lives

---

Home "Basement" Businesses

Some multi-level marketing (MLM) companies are legitimate and some aren't. I'll share both with you. If you are thinking about purchasing an MLM kit, you should read this first.

First, let's take the old pyramid scheme. This one works much like the well known chain letter, where you place your name on a letter with a list of other names and their addresses. Your name goes on the bottom of the list and you're asked to cross out the top name, send $X-amount of money to everyone on the list, and send your new list to ten additional people and sit back and wait for the cash to roll in. "Wait" is the key word. Most of the time those starting the letter are the only ones who benefit.

Just turn on your TV and you'll see another pyramid scam. It is one that has no product at all to sell. Members are asked to just "sell more memberships." See, everyone at the beginning makes large amounts of cash. However, the recruiting of new members peters out and the "pyramid" collapses. Instead of the win-win that's promised, it's only "few win"; while you lose. Avoid any plan that offers commissions based solely on recruiting of new members. Now, about more legitimate MLM companies.

These have one of their sales reps put together a "house party." They ask you to invite your family and friends. There are usually some type of refreshments provided, and then the pitch is given. The rep explains that the product being sold is in great demand and will save the consumer money. He will then motivate you by sharing his or other's success stories. If by now you don't have the general idea, here's the "trick."

"Pitchmen" tell you that by joining their company you will become rich. They tell you about the new car, the wife's new car, a $500,000 home, a lake home, and maybe even a pedigree dog. They'll even have pictures to prove it all! Could it be true? For them, yes. For you, maybe. Why? Because they have sales skills. It may be true for you, if you are also self-motivated. However, the ones I'm concerned about are those who really believe that the product will sell itself. An MLM kit will cost an individual anywhere from a couple of hundred dollars to several hundred dollars, and it will most likely end up in their basement or attic, collecting dust.

So, how can you avoid losing? It's not that difficult if you are a person who gives yourself the edge. That is, before you purchase a home-based business kit, go to the library and get some reading material on selling as a career. Read it. If you feel that you can do what it takes to become successful in sales then take your chance. However, the material you read on selling could give you more than a chance. And this is where I can give you some excellent advice. Infomercial time! Read, then commit to the principles laid down in **Simple Selling: Common Sense That Guarantees Your Success,** by yours truly. This book was written for individuals who want to <u>realize</u> <u>their</u> <u>dreams</u>. Do I believe you can succeed? Yes. The real question is, "Do you?"

You'll Pay For This!

There's a saying that has been kicked around by professors for years. It's "publish or perish." That is, if they don't write books or articles, then promotions and money seem to pass them by. When it comes to attempting to get a book published, my advice is simple. Learn as much as you can about writing, publishing, and marketing a book. Search the internet, library and by all means talk to authors who have been through the process. If you don't do this, then there's a good chance you will spend your time and money carelessly. Bottom line is that the book business has more than its fair share of money-grubbers who will take your money and even pass some of it on to someone else.

Here are a few ways you can get fleeced. "Vanity presses" can usually be spotted by their advertisements. They offer a free reading of your manuscript and "how to" advice in their fancy brochures. Now this is where you lose. First, they take no risk whether your book sells or not. Because just about everything they tell you, from printing, distribution, reviews, publicity, cover design, and editing—you pay for. Self-publishing is the road to take. It's true that you'll first have to do some research, and hard work, but in the end you'll save thousands of dollars on the services I mentioned above. Furthermore, you'll know the work is yours.

When I was a kid, I used to play cops and robbers. A couple of my favorite places to play were under the viaducts or around the railroad tracks. After all these years I can still remember seeing stacks of sale flyers from various stores that were thrown away by someone who was hired by the store to distribute them to residences. Many vanity presses work on the same principle; however, some are a little smarter. They rent warehouses then charge you storage for your books while they do <u>nothing</u>. So, if you decide to become a writer, don't use a vanity press.

I knew for years that the establishment was all about money. They even have bumper stickers that read, "The rat race is over. The rats won!" I used to think that certain institutions were exempt of "rats." That goes to show you how naive I was as a young man. Today, there's plenty of <u>selling of the soul</u>. I'm not selling college credits or telling students that they will secure high income jobs by obtaining a degree. Nor do most of us have anything to do with folks losing their hard earned money to unscrupulous religious organizations that have the needy themselves sending in their dollars to well-healed leaders for self-promotion. Why buy into the adage, "Get me once, it's your fault. Get me twice, it's mine."? You don't need to be "gotten" at all if you check REFERENCES. After all, <u>looking</u> like a good person is not necessarily being a good person.

PART V:

Keep Up Your Guard

The New York Times

August 19, 1999   *Barry Meier*

Metropolitan Life in Accord For Settlement of Fraud Suits

The Metropolitan Life Insurance Company, the nation's second-largest life insurer, agreed yesterday to pay hundreds of millions of dollars to settle lawsuits that had accused it of cheating customers through deceptive sales practices.

The settlement, which is subject to the approval of a Federal judge, would be the latest in a series of multimillion-dollar settlements by life insurers accused of fraud. ...

Your $$ Or Your Life!

Selling life insurance is something that I can easily explain to you. I sold life insurance door-to-door years ago. Basically there are two types of policies. One is term, the other whole life. All other policy plans derive from these two.

Term insurance is coverage that protects the policyholder from one point in time to another and has no cash value. The simplest way to illustrate this would be as follows: An individual purchases "a flight policy" at the airport. The policy would cover a frame of time, from Chicago to Los Angeles, for instance. Upon arrival, the policy terminates. Term insurance policies are also quite popular for covering home mortgages.

Whole life, on the other hand, builds up cash value. These policies can and are tailored by companies in many ways. Endowments, paid-up plans, Universal Life, etc. One of the major reasons people buy life insurance is to cover final expenses at the time of death. Term and whole life can be purchased individually or as a combination of both.

There are three major "tricks" an agent can "perform" for a policyholder. First, he can convince them to cash in their existing policy. Next, lie to them. And finally, out right cheat them. When a life insurance agent convinces an insured to cash surrender a policy for no reason other than to get them to buy another policy, it's sometimes referred to as "kicking out" a policy. An unscrupulous agent may replace an existing policy with his own, or convince you of an "in-force policy" that he happens to <u>discover</u> with another company. The reason this little scam is so unsavory is because it hurts the policyholder in a couple of ways.

When an agent convinces a policyholder to cash in their existing policy to purchase a new policy, three things happen: the insured loses all equity accumulated over the years; they are now buying life insurance at an older age, and this means that the new replacement policy will be higher in premium. Finally, the insured may discover that after their old policy has been cashed in, they are unable to purchase new insurance due to poor health or hazardous occupations, both of which neither existed before the agent convinced them to let their old policy "go." So be careful. "Kicking out" a policy can destroy your confidence to carry insurance at all.

To avoid being tricked by some greedy agent, I suggest you visit the library and read a simple book on life insurance. This should give you a better understanding as to what would be the best protection for you. Be wary of all agents that try to sell you saving and estate plans before the final expense fund is even taken care of. After all, it's really death insurance.

As a last thought, you might be thinking, "Don't the states have laws to protect us?" In a way, they do. Dishonest agents can and do lose their licenses and may even go to jail. Yet this is little justice for a family who is hurt financially.

I Owe! I Owe, I,...Ouch!

Be aware that finance companies making small loans using your personal property as collateral are distinguished from banks in several ways. First, they usually make riskier loans because they don't have the funds to make very large loans. Their interest rates are typically higher because they make loans that banks would typically turn down (i.e. an individual with a poor credit rating or with no solid collateral to secure the loan). Sometimes the finance companies' methods are shadier. They make risky loans at a high rate of interest to folks who have trouble making their payments on time, or even perhaps not at all. However, by constantly pressuring and threatening the borrower, the lender may eventually receive a payment plus a large penalty. Haven't you ever heard someone say: "I just want them off my back," or "What do I have to do to stop having them badger me?"

Let me give you an example. If you loan $10 to someone who agrees to pay you $20 back within two weeks, then after two weeks you only receive $15 (because they are "short"). What's your risk? You already made 50% on your original $10 loan! Plus, if you keep after them, you'll probably eventually get the other $5. And so it goes, if the rate of interest and penalty are high enough, your risk as a lender is not very much.

Others use pyramiding when contacting individuals contemplating bankruptcy, by convincing them to consolidate their loans into one monthly payment. For example, a borrower may have three separate loans of $1,000 with ABC Loan Company, $1,500 with XYZ Loan Company and $2,000 with a loan company who is attempting to get the borrower of <u>all</u> these loans to consolidate. Even though the borrower may be struggling to pay these existing loans, some finance companies will suggest that they consolidate all their loans into one with their company, thus making a *new* loan for a total of $4,500. To further entice you into this deal, they offer you a little additional money up front. Since a person will look for any means to avoid drowning with a sinking ship, these lenders are quite successful. Because a borrower is already financially "strapped," it is very difficult for him to make the new payment. Some will, but only after being harassed by phone or in person by a "chaser," one who threatens to repossess the borrower's personal property, take them to court, etc. Nice job, eh? Other folks have to file for Chapter 11 or 7. In order to avoid being named in a bankruptcy, a finance company may ask the borrower to file a "partial bankruptcy." Therefore, by not being included in the bankruptcy case, the finance company can continue to demand payment on their loan. How do they sweeten the deal? By offering the borrower a little more money.

So first, don't bite off more than you can chew. If you still aren't convinced, then I suggest you make certain that the person or business you intend on borrowing from is fair, honest and understanding. How does one do this? By asking around and getting references. You can even check with your local Better Business Bureau, or your State Banking Authorities.

Caveat Emptor

What are "bogus" billings? Here's an example. Your business is sent what appears to be an invoice for Yellow Page advertising. You may just send off your check to the address on the statement. However, you should scrutinize every invoice you receive, because you just might see in fine print on the invoice a disclaimer that reads: "This is not an official invoice. This is a solicitation."

These "invoices" are often sent to us as well. A person I know was sent a survey in the mail. For her effort in completing the survey, she was offered a free copy of a magazine about cats. After completing and mailing the survey, she received an invoice billing her for a year's subscription to the magazine. She then had to take the time to write a letter advising them that she was not interested in a subscription, only her "free" copy. The tip here? If you receive any books or magazines through the mail, and you didn't request them, it's not your responsibility to pay for or to return them. That's the chance the sender is taking. Sometimes solicitors will follow-up invoices with threats about turning you over to a collection agency, or to their legal department. Do you think this scam will ever quit? No. After all, there's always more than one way to "skin a cat."

Here's another bad deal: mailing lists targeting college bound students that advertise "free" grant money for school. Since most parents would like to see their children go to college, they are easy "marks" for this scam. It works like this. You pay $X amount of money, let's say $1,000. The company soliciting you by mail will then send you a list of organizations that supposedly hand out grant money for college tuition. They will even give you "references" to call if you feel the need to check them out. The references will be fake too. When you receive your list, many of the phone numbers on the list are disconnected. The organizations don't or never did exist. If they do exist, the criteria for qualifying for receiving the grant money is next to impossible to satisfy. Another trick, to extract money out of you.

Therefore if you are included in the millions who have received an offer of some sort, whether it's locating your family's genealogy or being "honored" by being placed in **Who's Who,** remember the old warning: "Let the buyer beware!"

www.computerscams.HELP!!!

On more than one occasion, I've heard computer salespersons referred to as the "used car salesmen of the technological age." Having purchased many a computer in my time, I believe this description is not so far off.

The automobile has been around for about 100 years, which has given us enough time to "figure out" how these machines work. Probably more importantly, however, is that we've also had 100 years to "figure out" the people who sell them. Yes...that infamous car salesman! Computers, on the other hand, are relatively "new" to us, having a history which spans only about 25 years or so. With all of the rapid advances in technology, the computer buyer faces a real challenge when it comes to avoiding some of the "dirty little tricks" that have infiltrated this ever-changing industry.

In many states, one needs a license to sell real estate, sell insurance, or even to repair a television. But to sell or repair a computer, you need only to rent a store front, hang out your sign, and you're in business. Never has *caveat emptor* meant more than when it comes to buying computer-related goods and services. Here are a few of the computer schemes I've encountered.

An ad in the newspaper showed a PC with a 500MHz processor selling for 20% *less* than a PC with a 400MHz processor. What a great deal! Both systems included the exact same items; monitor, printer, and software. Each package had everything I needed to be up and running. However, after careful examination of the ad (and in small print I might add), I discovered that the 500MHz system had a *less* powerful processor than the 400MHz system. To put it in terms that may be better understood, the 500MHz system had a V-6 engine and the 400MHz system had a V-8 in it. At first glance, all I saw was the *speed,* not the type of processor. In the end, the 400MHz PC was more suited to the tasks that I needed the system to perform. As always, be sure to read the fine print!

Another "trick" to watch out for is the proprietary hardware game. Some personal computers are designed such that only those components that come from the original manufacturer will work on the machine. And most likely those components are astronomically priced. Heaven forbid that you'd own one of these machines and ever want to enhance it!

How about those "free" color printers that come with some systems? Did you know that combining red, green, and blue ink makes black? If you didn't, you'll soon find out when you have to buy a new color cartridge at $20^{00} a pop. A black only cartridge costs about $5^{00}. It doesn't take long to figure out why the color printer is "free." The manufacturer knows they're going to make all their profit selling you new color ink cartridges.

As with many electronic products today, computer manufacturers offer extended warranties—you know, the extra couple of years guarantee on part or unit replacement. However, give this some thought when it comes to your personal computer. Computer technology is so rapidly changing that you may have a "dinosaur" PC within just a few short years. Why extend the warranty? Save your money for the newer, up-to-date model which will probably be available in a few months.

Tick, Tick, Tick...

A blind rabbit and a blind snake meet each other. Neither one remembers what kind of animal they are, so they decide to feel each other. The rabbit says, "You feel me first." The snake says: "Okay," and he starts feeling the rabbit. He says, "Well, you have fur all over, and a little cotton tail, and two long ears, and big back feet."

The rabbit says, "I know! I'm a rabbit! Yippee!" Then the rabbit feels the snake.

He says, "Okay, you're long and thin, and slimy all over, and there's a little forked tongue." The snake says, "Damn, I'm a lawyer."

"The first thing we do, let's kill all the Lawyers" [Henry VI, Part 2 (1592) act 4, sc. 2, l. [73]]—that's what Shakespeare wrote. Volumes have been written on bad attorneys, and bad jokes about them are in the hundreds. Just keep one thing in mind when you hire a lawyer: they use time to their benefit.

For example, most of us are always anxious to get our legal problems settled quickly, or better sooner than later. If you retain a cunning lawyer, the only "quick" you'll see is how fast your money will dwindle away while your attorney "sits" on your file. Understand, the more time they spend on your "file" with you, other attorneys, on the phone, on the golf course, etc., the more they can bill you. So as you can very well figure, when it comes to taking an abundance of time getting a legal matter settled, it's to their advantage and your expense. Will Rogers said: ("I went down and spoke at some lawyer's meeting last night. They didn't think much of my little squib about driving the shysters out of their profession. They seemed to...doubt just who would have to leave").

Here are three ways to avoid hiring a lawyer

without worrying about paying for wasted time. First, contingency. This is where the attorney gets a percentage of the settlement from a lawsuit. Second, pay a flat fee for services rendered, regardless of time spent. Third, only pick a lawyer based upon a good recommendation. I use only three examples because: "You may fool some of the people some of the *time;* you can even fool some of the people all of the *time;* but you can't fool all the people all of the *time*" (Alexander K. McClure, <u>Lincoln's</u> <u>Yarns</u> <u>and</u> <u>Stories</u> (1904); also attributed to Phineas Barnum). I guess there ain't a way that we won't fool none of the people none of the *time!*

If you want a win/win situation, ask the attorney a lot of questions at your first "free" consultation with them. Plus, you will need references. Ask a friend or relative. You can even check with your local Bar Association. Forget about what William Shakespeare wrote about lawyers. However, make certain you don't retain one that likes to "kill" your time.

One last joke for you: "Man goes to a lawyer for help."

MAN: "What is your least expensive fee?"

LAWYER: "$50 for three questions."

MAN: "That's pretty expensive, isn't it?"

LAWYER: "Yes. So what's your third question?"

Four Of A Kind

This chapter took quite a bit of thought on my part to write. It's difficult to explain in just a few pages what can't even be figured out in volumes of books. Let me get right to the point. It's the real question we are asking ourselves in this book. Who are the biggest crooks?

INSURANCE EXECUTIVES?

IN THE NEWS   THE WALL STREET JOURNAL.

Friday, August 20, 1999   *Associated Press News Service*

Motorists File Suits Against Three Big Insurers

Seven Maryland motorists are seeking $300 million in damages from three of the nation's largest insurance companies for allegedly cheating policyholders out of millions in personal-injury protection benefits. ...

PHYSICIANS?

IN THE NEWS   **The New York Times**

October 16, 1998

Doctor Is Charged With Health Care Fraud

A prominent Park Avenue doctor and an anesthesiologist who worked with him were indicted yesterday on charges that they lied about fertility surgeries to win insurance coverage for their patients. ...

... Both were charged with conspiracy, health care fraud and mail fraud in connection with an alleged 10-year scheme to falsely bill fertility surgeries that were not covered by insurance as gynecological surgeries that were. ...

ATTORNEYS?

IN THE NEWS   **THE WALL STREET JOURNAL.**

Friday, August 26, 1994   *Amy Stevens*

A List of Bad Lawyers To Go On Line

A list of lawyers who have run afoul of the law will soon be available on line.

The American Bar Association's National Discipline Data Bank — 25,000 lawyers' names, addresses, aliases and violations — will be available at the touch of a button. ...

POLITICIANS?

The New York Times

September 25, 1999   *Mike Allen*

Investigation of Kickbacks Is Believed to Be Widening

Paul J. Silvester, the former Connecticut State Treasurer who has pleaded guilty to taking kickbacks, is providing Federal Investigators with detailed information about possibly illegal payments to politicians in an attempt to dramatically cut his prison time, according to officials and lawyers involved in the investigations.

Prosecutors are said to be focusing on Connecticut politicians from both major parties who received payments — variously referred to as finders' fees, consulting fees and placement fees — from investment firms in return for being entrusted with determining where to invest state pension funds, but did little or no work to earn those fees. ...

It's time I explain a little about the property and casualty business. Just so you're clear on what they do, I'll start out by reminding you that they are the ones who sell and service insurance policies on your homes, vehicles, and businesses. They sell insurance on anything other than your life or health. It's not only *coverage* that most people don't understand, but

159

also the payment of claims.

"The other day my house caught fire." My claim adjuster said, "Shouldn't be a problem. What kind of coverage do you have?" I said, "Fire and theft." The adjuster frowned, "Uh oh. Wrong kind. Should be fire OR theft." Two of the most famous phrases that come out of an agent's mouth are: "You're covered" or "You're not covered for that."

I can remember when my car was hit while it was parked, unattended, on a side street by my office. I called the insurance company of the driver who had damaged my car. In my mind, it was a clear case of negligence. What do you think they told me? They said there would be no payment on their insured's behalf because it was an "act of God." That's right. It appears that their insured advised them that he had been stung by a bee and that caused him to run into my car. Only after hiring an attorney, did his company pay up. In fact, it cost the insurance company an extra $1,500 because they were responsible for my lawyer's bill: his typing a letter stating what I had already reported.

For a good number of years, the above FOUR OF A KIND were happy doing business together. Lawyers who don't work for insurance companies work <u>with</u> them. Doctors just send in bills for their services. But things have changed. Since law suits and medical costs have been on an astronomical rise during the past quarter of a century, *loyalties have shifted.* Many lawyers and doctors have simply jumped ship. One reason is that they don't care much for the idea that insurance people set their fees, or should I say they believe they set their fees too low. You see, once upon a time everyone was happy. Mainly because everyone was making money. Insurance companies were not worrying about legal fees or doctor's bills. The lawyers didn't have as much competition from their own colleagues so ambulance chasing was kept to a minimum. Furthermore, there were many sad stories popping up about people getting taken by insurance companies. You know the tales. Someone getting seriously injured and a claims adjuster getting them to sign off the claim for "chicken feed" when, in fact, they should have been paid hundreds of thousands of dollars more due to the disabling nature of their injuries. Then, of course, those disheartening stories about the lawyer who sends his client to an underhanded doctor who treats a healthy person as an injured one in order to increase the chances of a fatter settlement from the insurance company. Old greed took over.

Now everyone is unhappy. Lawyers are suing insurance companies. It's like the dog that bites the hand that feeds it. Doctors have their own "beef." They don't like HMO's. Who does? While the insurance industry continues to point their fingers at anyone but themselves, out of one side of their mouth they say it's lawsuits that run up insurance premiums. Out of the other side, insurance companies blame doctors for over-charging, double billing, and unnecessary costs. Insurance executives also blame their own insureds, agents, and even each other for high costs and losses. What is the answer to such a growing problem?

Some people say take insurance out of the private sector and let the government control it. Talk about scary. They actually want <u>politicians</u> to protect our money? That would be like a hungry German Shepherd guarding a pound of raw ground beef. No people, I don't have a good answer for this one, nor do I know who is doing more thieving. It's a toss up.

However, since most of the FOUR OF A KIND have been fighting over profits and power, you may have a chance to get <u>your</u> <u>claim</u> settled in the fair and speedy manner you've been promised.

SUMMARY:

Time's Up!

You and I are now at the end, or what we sales reps like to call, *the close.* Two things I want to be sure that you know: First, that I have met your needs, and second, that my purpose here is clear. I know I will be able to accomplish both by sharing the answers to these questions:

1. What is *noblesse oblige?*

2. Why "The Mask?"

Noblesse oblige is a term from the Middle Ages. It means that being privileged entails certain responsibilities. In my mind, it has always meant that those <u>with</u> owe it to those <u>without</u>, to extend a helping hand. We all, at times, have an opportunity to share our knowledge. To me, life is not like a play that one is able to rehearse over and over. Each moment, once lived, is never duplicated. We all make mistakes; however, each of us has the opportunity to try our best and help our fellow man. Even if at times, we find it difficult to love our neighbor, we should at least tolerate them. When all is said and done, you and I should be able to say: "I did it the right way!"

As you have seen, "The Mask" represents disguise or concealment. When someone is masked, it is hard to tell who the person is or what is being concealed. I think most of us, at times, have told a "little white lie"—something that won't hurt someone. The lie may even have been to make a person feel better, like: "What a nice tie!" or "What a great looking dress!" And in your mind you're thinking: "Wow! <u>Who</u> sold them <u>that</u>?" However, when a product or service is masked so well that it can cause financial loss or even loss of life, then it should be exposed.

Yet one of the hardest things for people to do is <u>unmask</u> their thoughts. For instance, when you are being told about a product or service, and you have questions about something, you remain silent. Maybe because you're too shy to speak up. It could be you think you will sound foolish. If you are afraid to ask a doctor, lawyer, insurance agent, or anyone about their fees, you must

MAKE yourself ask! Speak what's on your mind. There's no such thing as a silly question. Remember, no one knows everything and everyone knows something that no one else knows.

Salespeople who look honest, but ain't, can and do cause much grief. Many times the grief is more than just financial loss. It's mental anguish. It's true, people, in general, do tend to judge a book by its cover, but keep in mind it's only a book. It's impossible to judge an individual by their appearance. What you see on the outside isn't necessarily what's inside. It's always best to get a referral when dealing with a new business acquaintance. A time or two ago, folks shook hands to finalize a promise, commitment, or even a business deal. Today, we've moved way past the hand shake. Now it's a fast-paced business environment with lengthy legal contracts full of "whereas's" and "where is's." "Take care of yourself because no one else will," has been emphasized too much. I still have great hopes and dreams; however, I act with more caution now. If everything was perfect in the business and political world, I wouldn't have written this book. Since almost everyone is a salesperson, we need to pay careful attention to our everyday relationships.

Understandably, I haven't been able to write about each and every business or profession. Unfortunately, that would require volumes. Instead, my purpose was to offer you a quick and helpful guide to some of the more common scams. That doesn't mean that you shouldn't keep your eyes peeled for the ones I've missed. Remember to apply your common sense with the ones I've shared. You'll do just fine!

There are some outstanding salespeople in this world. Without question, there are many honest ones. However, when it comes to money, many times greed takes over. Then the temptation to look for a fast and *masked* buck becomes hard to resist. In the end, your integrity should stand above all else and never be for sale.

My hope is that you have enjoyed this book. I'm confident it has made you a better consumer. For those who read this book and haven't always done the "right" thing, perhaps you will start now. After all, it's just as easy to become successful by being fair. You have my heartfelt gratitude for spending some of your irreplaceable <u>time</u> with me.

IT'S A **JUNGLE** OUT THERE !!!

Index

A

B

D

E

F

Food. *See* Groceries; Meat
Forms
    tips for dealing with, 53, 86, 124
Furniture, 100–102

G

Games
    hardware, 151–152
Gasoline, 96–99
Generic brands
    in batteries, 27–28
Goals. *See* Buying goals
Greed, 33, 162
Grief
    avoiding, 6, 8
Groceries, 65–70, 99
Ground beef, 68–69
Guides
    fishing, 70–75

H

Hardware games
    proprietary, 151–152
Health care, 84–87. *See also* Physicians
    fraud in, 84, 158
Health insurance, 84–86. *See also* HMO's
Heater repair, 103–105
HMO's, 162
Home-based businesses, 131–135
Home buying, 33–37, 57–61
    "falling in love," 37
Home inspection, 81–84
Honesty, 15–16, 103, 138

K

L

M

MLS. *See* Multiple Listing Services
Money
    losing, 7–8, 15–16, 55–56
    saving, 5–6, 21–22
Mortgages
    re-financing, 129
Motel rooms
    booking, 49–50
Multi-level marketing (MLM), 131–135
Multiple Listing Services (MLS), 34

N

Name brands
    in batteries, 27–28
New York Stock Exchange, 88
New York Times, 33, 53, 81, 88, 103, 140, 158–159
Noblesse oblige, 166–167

O

"Off" brands
    in batteries, 27–28
Oil changes, 126–128
Original parts, 112–114
Overbooking, 48
Overpaying
    in home buying, 36

P

Packaged travel, 41
Packaging, 32
Paint jobs
    for automobiles, 110–111

Penny stocks, 88
Phone service, 115–120
Physicians, 158, 161–163
    scheduling office visits, 18
    selecting, 13–14
Politicians
    tricks of, 159, 163
Prices
    inflated, 64
Printers
    "free," 152
Proprietary hardware games, 151–152
Publishing business, 135–138
Pyramid schemes, 131–132

Q

Questions
    asking, 81

R

Radio marketing, 1–2
Real estate, 33–37
Receipts, 97–99
"Red Book" for automobiles, 13
"Red eye" flights, 48
References
    checking, 138, 148–149
Referrals
    securing, 37, 44, 58, 105, 111, 128, 146, 155
Religious scams, 137–138
Rental cars, 51–53
    insuring, 52–53
"Reproduction" costs
    of x-rays, 41